The Formation of
American Local Governments

Oxford University Press

Oxford   New York   Toronto
Delhi   Bombay   Calcutta   Madras   Karachi
Kuala Lumpur   Singapore   Hong Kong   Tokyo
Nairobi   Dar es Salaam   Cape Town
Melbourne   Auckland   Madrid

and associated companies in
Berlin   Ibadan

Library of Congress Cataloging-in-Publication Data
Burns, Nancy, 1964–
The formation of American local governments : private values in
public institutions / Nancy Burns.
p. cm.   Includes bibliographical references and index.
ISBN 0–19–508275–3 — ISBN 0-19-509093-4 (pbk.)
1. Local government—United States.
2. Municipal government—United States.   3. Special districts—United States.
4. Quality of life—United States.   I. Title.
JS341.B87   1994
320.8'0973—dc20   93–46100

3 5 7   6 4 2
Printed in the United States of America
on acid-free paper

For the memory of my mother

BABS BRANYAN BURNS

December 13, 1936
White Plains, Georgia
May 26, 1990
Sardis, Mississippi

ACKNOWLEDGMENTS

I have been able to take advantage of the wisdom of many different people over the course of my work on this project.

At Harvard, I was fortunate to work with Gary King, Paul Peterson, Kay Lehman Schlozman, and Sidney Verba. They helped me through the first incarnation of this work. Discussions with Jonathan Simon have helped me think more clearly. Michael Dawson and John Jackson read and commented on parts of the work. Glenn Beamer, Doug Dion, Gerald Gamm (and the students in his graduate seminar on urban politics at the University of Rochester), Don Herzog, Paul Schumaker, and Scott Zeleznik read all of it. Their comments were invaluable. David Roll, my editor at Oxford, made a series of crucial suggestions that improved the work significantly. I am particularly grateful for the energy he put into the manuscript. Jim Alt, Jo Andrews, Bob Axelrod, Babs Branyan Burns, Sydney Burns, Matt Dickinson, Stephen Elkin, Arnold Fleischmann, Stephan Haggard, Dennis Judd, Terry McDonald, H. W. Perry, Mark Peterson, Debbie Snow, and the two anonymous reviewers for Oxford University Press also made important criticisms and suggestions. Of course, the errors are my responsibility.

Paul Schumaker is responsible for developing and encouraging my interest in local politics. Sidney Verba helped develop further my interest in questions of participation, equality, and representation by involving me generously in his own work.

Dwayne Bey helped make the data for parts of Chapter 1 and Chapter 5 accessible. Anita McDermott typed the bibliography. Amy Englehart entered parts of the data for my pretests. An NSF graduate fellowship and substantial financial assistance from the Harvard University Department of Government provided me with the space to explore the idea. The University of Michigan Department of Political Science and the Center for Political Studies at the Institute for Social Research provided me with the time and support to complete it.

My mother provided the inspiration for the work. Gary King helped channel it. Scott Zeleznik helped sustain it.

CONTENTS

The Formation of
American Local Governments

1

Private Values, Public Institutions

The village or township is the only association which is so perfectly natural that, wherever a number of men are collected, it seems to constitute itself . . . it is man who makes monarchies and establishes republics, but the township seems to come from the hand of God.

ALEXIS DE TOCQUEVILLE

SENATOR KENNEDY: But are you not the mayor of all the people in Los Angeles?

MAYOR YORTY: Of the people of the city of Los Angeles, yes.

KENNEDY: Then if they have a problem, do they not look to you for some leadership?

YORTY: Yes. . . . But whether or not I can solve a problem may depend on my jurisdiction.

SENATOR RIBICOFF: As I listened to your testimony, Mayor Yorty, I made some notes. This morning you have really waived authority and responsibility in the following areas: schools, welfare, transportation, employment, health, and housing, which leaves you as the head of the city basically with a ceremonial function, police, and recreation.

YORTY: That is right, and fire.[1]

Americans continually create new local governments—new cities and new special district governments. Over the course of the past 350 years, Americans have formed almost 50,000 cities and special districts. The reasons they have done so and the arrangements that have enabled them to succeed illuminate the place of local government in American politics, point to the importance of the boundaries and politics that these citizens have created, and describe the values that they have embedded in these new institutions.[2]

3

Special Districts and Cities

In contrast to cities, special districts are independent local governments that generally perform only a few local government functions. They can tax, float bonds, and provide services. They are not accountable to other governments. They might be housing authorities, water districts, port authorities, or municipal utility districts, for example. Generally, they perform one single function. These governments have territorial boundaries. However, they have geographic flexibility that other governments do not have. They can overlap other governments. As a consequence of this flexibility, for example, all parts of Cook County, Illinois, have at least two layers of special districts; some parts of the county have seven.[3] One government might provide water service, another garbage pick-up, another bus service, and so on. There is no requirement that the layered governments have similar boundaries. Cities or municipalities (I will use the terms interchangeably) are, by contrast, general purpose local governments. They generally provide a broader range of services than do special districts. I describe the specific procedures required to create these new governments in Appendix A.

The Significance of Creating Governments

Citizens have created more local governments in the twentieth century than they did when settling the West or the Midwest—or the East, for that matter (Figure 1.1).[4] In the last fifty years, the large majority of these new governments have been special districts, not cities (Table 1.1).

   These local governments were not created in any immediately discernible pattern among the states (Figures 1.2 and 1.3). The creation of new governments is not a natural consequence of something as straightforward as population increase. A close look at the maps underlines this point. Citizens of states with similar populations and with what we might have thought were similar reasons to exercise a habit of forming governments acted in dissimilar ways. Citizens of North Dakota formed more cities than did citizens of South Dakota. Alabamans formed more special districts than did Georgians. Citizens of Maine and Vermont formed cities, whereas citizens of the other New England states largely did not. Citizens of a few states—Illinois, Indiana, Massachusetts, New Jersey, and Pennsylvania—formed an exceedingly large number of special districts.

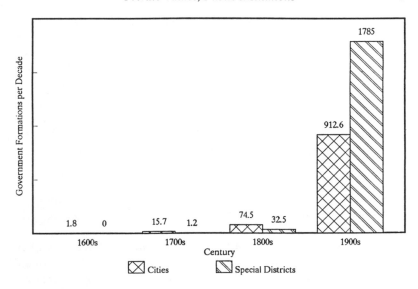

Fig. 1.1. Government formations per decade in a given century.

If the creation of local governments is not simply a mechanical response to population increases or shifts, what drives their formation? We can begin to answer this question if we recognize that the process is a political one and if we consider that even after 350 years, efforts to form cities and special districts remain time-consuming, prone to failure, and expensive. Given these hurdles, only certain individuals and certain kinds of groups will have the interest and the resources necessary to succeed in these formation efforts. Businesses—developers and manufacturers—have led many of these efforts within the incentive structures defined by state and federal governments. In so doing, these businesses have created congenial regulatory climates, congenial tax climates, and mechanisms for increasing the value of land at slim cost to developers. In the process, these businesses have enabled middle- and upper-middle-class citizens to acquire services, to keep their taxes low, to wall out the poor, and to indulge their taste for racial exclusion.

I will argue that without businesses, citizens with these concerns about services, low taxes, and exclusion would have been much less successful in institutionalizing their values in American local government. With this business support, cities—and, to a lesser extent, special districts—

Table 1.1.   Number of Municipalities, Special Districts, Townships, and Counties in the United States, 1942–1987

Type	1942	1952	1962	1972	1987
Municipalities	16,220	16,807	18,000	18,517	19,200
Special districts	8,299	12,340	18,323	23,885	29,532
Counties	3,050	3,052	3,043	3,044	3,042
Townships	18,919	17,202	17,142	16,991	16,691

Source: McFeeley, 1978; U.S. Department of Commerce, 1987, Census of Governments, v. 1, p. xvi.

provide boundaries for races, classes, service provision, and taxation. In so doing, these boundaries define politics and provide meaning to American citizenship.

To begin to build the foundation for this argument we must develop an understanding of the kinds of political choices people make when they create cities and special districts. That understanding requires an awareness of the major differences between the two in terms of powers, services, participation, accountability, and finance. I will start the discussion there. Afterwards, in the final section of this chapter, I will outline my arguments about the impact of these choices and political forces on American local government.

Legend

1 Dot = 1 New City

Fig. 1.2.   New cities, 1952–87 (randomly distributed within states).

Fig. 1.3. New special districts, 1952–87 (randomly distributed within states).

The Consequences of Institutional Choices

The boundaries that citizens draw when they create special districts and cities matter in American politics because they define the limits of particular arrangements of political power, particular kinds of service provision, certain characteristics of political participation and political accountability, and certain arrangements for funding the work of local government. In so doing, these new governments provide boundaries that define citizenship and embody values ranging from antitax sentiments to racial exclusion. In America, we have given local governments enough autonomy that this local citizenship has meaning.

Some cities have little public housing. Some cities provide mass transit. Some cities have high taxes. Some cities have exclusively white residents. Some cities have large tax bases. Some places are governed largely by special districts. For some people, buying a house illuminates the differences between localities.[5] For others, the search for a job or for affordable housing provides equally powerful illumination. The differences between Kansas City, Missouri, and Kansas City, Kansas; Memphis and Germantown; Los Angeles and Pasadena; Detroit and Grosse Pointe; Boston and Brookline; Washington, D.C., and Arlington provide indications of the meaning of limits.

Part of the reason that these boundaries matter is illuminated by the distinction between institutions and governments. I use the term *institutions* in a very specific manner.[6] The stable *institutions* of local government are the laws created by state legislatures and sometimes modified by the federal government that define the powers of local government. Local *governments*, then, are bundles of particular *institutions*—for example, the power to zone, the power to tax, and the power to provide services. I will argue later that when people try to form new local governments, what they really want is access to these institutions. A more familiar case should help to clarify my use of the term *institution*. A politician who wins an election for president of the United States gains access to and control over the powers (the institutions), the legally defined capabilities, of that office. Similarly, the people who succeed in creating a new local government gain access to and control over the powers of local government. These powers, the *institutions* that compose the *governments*, are crucial for understanding both the politics of goverment creation and the politics that occur once the government is created.

The following sections describe the institutions that compose special districts and municipalities and begin to suggest why citizens have believed these institutions desirable enough to exert time and energy to form new governments. In addition, the discussion begins to point to the role that states have played in defining and redefining the bundles of institutions that compose these governments.

Powers

These governments and their geographical boundaries define the availability of bundles of local governmental powers. The crucial powers of special districts are the power to tax and charge fees, the power to issue debt, and the power to appropriate private land for public use (eminent domain). Municipalities have the same powers as do special districts, with one important addition—the power to define citizenship through zoning (since 1916) and through residential inspection (from the 1600s through the 1830s). The powers to tax and issue debt enable special districts and municipalities to provide services to their residents and to build infrastructure. The power to zone means that municipalities can define who and what can and cannot reside within their boundaries, in some instances conferring economic and racial meaning on those boundaries.[7]

Of course, these powers have changed over time as states, the federal government, and ambitious individuals have defined and redefined cities and special districts to suit their own purposes. These definitions and redefinitions have changed the meaning of the boundaries and the content of the politics.

Services

These governments provide services and facilities, including water service, mass transit, sewerage, stadiums, nursing homes, libraries, hospitals, gas service, police, fire protection, electric service, landfills, and airports. Living in one city as opposed to another or within the boundaries of a special district means that certain kinds and levels of services will or will not be available. The governments and their boundaries demarcate these differences.

In recent years, citizens have been forming cities that provide few services (Figure 1.4). Older cities provide services that we generally associate with city governments. Of the 17,397 cities in the United States reporting their service involvement in 1987, 2,000 cities provide *none*

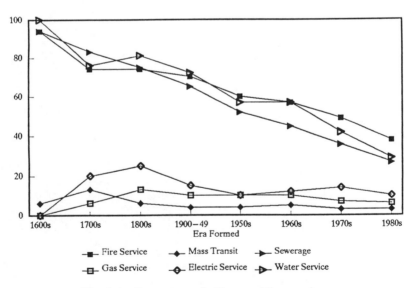

Fig. 1.4. Percentage of cities providing services.

of the services noted (Table 1.2). Another 2,000 provide only one service. And 3,000 more provide only two of the services examined. In addition, older cities spend significantly more money per capita on health services, hospitals, and police services than do newer cities.[8] Part of the significance of the municipal boundaries, then, is that they define differential availability of public services. Moreover, the fact that new cities provide very few services hints at the possibility that citizens who created these new governments probably did not do so in order to gain access to new services.

Special districts provide many of the services that we often associate with municipalities (Table 1.3). Indeed, the services once supplied by cities are increasingly supplied by special districts. In addition, special districts provide a number of services that cities often do not, for example, air pollution control and soil conservation services.

Table 1.2.   Number of Services Provided
by Municipalities, 1987

Number of Services*	Number of Municipalities†
0	1942
1	2098
2	2875
3	3463
4	2857
5	1877
6	1199
7	604
8	240
9	79
10	48
11	38
12	77

*The services include water service, mass transit, sewerage, stadiums, nursing homes, libraries, hospitals, gas service, fire protection, electric service, landfills, and airports. There is one particularly important service that this figure does not consider: police service. For a description of variations in police service across cities, see Herbert Jacob, "Policy Responses to Crime," in Paul E. Peterson, ed., *The New Urban Reality* (Washington, D.C.: Brookings Institution, 1985), pp. 225–252.

†A total of 17,397 cities, or 90.6% of all cities, reported their service involvement in the 1987 Census of Government Survey.

Table 1.3. Special District Functions, 1987

Function	Number	Percent Increase Since 1977
Natural resources	6,360	−3.6
Fire protection	5,070	21.1
Housing and community development	3,464	43.9
Water supply	3,060	23.4
Cemeteries	1,627	0.7
Sewerage	1,607	−0.2
Parks and recreation	1,004	21.1
Libraries	830	41.6
Hospitals	783	9.5
Education*	713	−30.1
Highways	621	−4.8
Health	484	38.3
Airports	369	23.4
Other†	1,489	66.2
Multiple-function Districts	2,051	19.2

*Primarily school building authorities.

†Includes parking facilities; water transport and terminals; solid waste disposal; gas; electric, and public transit utilities; industrial development and mortgage credit; and other single-function districts.

Source: U.S. Census of Governments, v. 1, 1989:xi.

Accountability and Participation

These governments create structures of accountability and political participation for American local politics. Living within one set of governmental institutions and boundaries as opposed to another affects the ways in which citizens can and do involve themselves in local politics. The distinctive rules for public involvement for special districts and cities compose part of the institutional structure of local government.

When citizens form special districts, they define the character of accountability and relevant local political participation in several ways. These special district governments are independent institutions that are nominally accountable to citizens and not accountable to other local, state, or federal governments. Because these layers of government can have different boundaries, they create varying communities for political participation. Two neighbors might be in the same transit district but in different water districts, housing districts, and economic development districts.

Simply living in one of these districts and being of a particular age does not qualify an American citizen to participate in the district's politics. Unlike other kinds of governments, special districts can have property qualifications for voters. In 1973, the Supreme Court ruled that special districts are exempt from the one-person, one-vote requirement placed on other governments.[9] Moreover, there are sometimes no residence requirements for voters in special district elections, thus allowing people who own property in the district to vote even if they live elsewhere.[10] Sometimes, too, there are odd mixes of requirements.[11]

Special districts do not engender broad participation in politics. As Perrenod notes:

> the bond election [for the Greenwood, Texas, Utility District, in 1969, to authorize $2.5 million in bonds and corresponding taxes] was held at the development sales office, and the proposition authorizing the bond issuance and the levy of taxes to pay the principal and interest was *unanimously approved by the four persons who voted in the election.*[12]

Participation can reach levels as high as 50% or as low as 5% in the formation elections, but after formation 2–5% is an unusually high turnout.[13] Sometimes, however, special districts fail to hold elections because the special district officials do not know when or if the elections are supposed to occur![14]

These findings of low levels of participation are not surprising given the difficulty of even locating the boundaries of special districts. One author notes that "without the benefit of surveying or cartography background, district location, even by county, is not available [at least in Arizona]."[15] Another author points out that the "Florida agency charged with special district monitoring . . . still has no master list of districts in that state."[16]

My own search for the special districts in the county where I lived when I began this study (Middlesex County, Massachusetts) was a complete failure. I spoke with all of the local government offices in the "blue government pages" of the Boston area telephone book, none of whom could tell me the boundaries of the special districts in Middlesex County and none of whom could even tell me the names of the districts that governed me. I spoke with the city planner, the county planner, and the state planner. All of the planners said that it would only take a few phone calls for me to learn the boundaries of the districts; it is unclear to me where else I should have called. The one bona fide special district government office with which I spoke denied being a government and assured me that it was only an agency.

The way in which the board members are selected in special districts also affects accountability. While city councils and other city officials are usually chosen in elections, members of governing boards of special districts are either elected or appointed. Appointment processes do not necessarily include consideration of citizens' opinions. As one central Pennsylvania borough council argued in 1989, "publicly discussing candidates could deter people from applying for the jobs."[17] Election to these boards likewise does not ensure accountability. Members of special district government boards tend to run without opposition.[18] In 1957 Bollens wrote that

> a widespread practice has developed among board members who obtain office on an elective basis. A member who has decided not to seek reelection resigns before the election so that his successor, often selected by the remainder of the board membership, can run as the incumbent.[19]

Municipalities also establish communities of participation. Participation in city politics varies immensely. Average turnout is about 31% in municipal elections and has been falling since the 1930s.[20] In some city elections, voting turnout can reach as high as 61%.[21]

Establishing a special district defines the boundaries for relevant communities of participation and constructs a rather nonparticipatory politics. Establishing a municipality also defines the boundaries of relevant communities of participation and can construct a range of forms of politics, from participatory to less participatory. Levels of participation in municipal politics, however, are generally much higher than in special district politics.

In addition, the boundaries created confer citizenship upon some and not upon others. Living within the boundaries of a municipality almost always grants one citizenship in that municipality, the right to vote and to enjoy the privileges the city affords its citizens. Living within the boundaries of a special district does not necessarily confer citizenship in that district. Thus, forming a new special district or city means choosing a probable level of citizen involvement.

Financing

Creating a government also means defining access to certain forms of public finance and signifies the character of local taxes—who pays and how much. Special districts provide a different form of local public finance than do municipal governments. The crucial differences are that special districts issue different kinds of bonds than do municipalities, that special districts rely much less on property taxes than do municipalities, and that special districts receive distinct forms of federal aid. Because the financing mechanisms of special districts are not common knowledge, I will briefly discuss the financing of special districts in general.

Special Districts. Special districts have a variety of revenue sources (Tables 1.4 and 1.5). They receive a smaller proportion of their total revenue from property taxes than do cities (8%). More of their revenue comes from federal, state, and local governments (22%), from user charges (30%), and from utility revenues (27%).[22] In addition, some states exempt special districts from the revenue, debt, and expenditure limits they place on other forms of local government.[23]

In 1986–1987, special district outstanding debt at the end of the fiscal year was $*137 billion*, up significantly from $5.8 billion in 1957.[24] Of this amount, 120 billion was nonguaranteed debt. (Nonguaranteed debt

Table 1.4.   Special District Revenues in $Millions

Sources	1986–7	1981–2	1971–2
Federal government	5,763	4,405	1,550
State government	1,951	1,810	208
Local governments	3,069	2,057	538
Property taxes	3,862	2,266	903
General sales taxes and gross receipts	1,541	534	41
Other taxes	88	45	8
Charges	14,276	8,714	2,228
Special assessments	454	300	84
Sale of property	66	78	23
Interest earnings	3,528	2,501	239
Other	2,523	1,094	103
Utility revenue	13,115	6,940	1,592
Employee retirement revenue	416	217	40

Source: U.S. Census of Governments, v. 4, 1982:1, v. 4, 1987:1.

Table 1.5. Federal Aid per Dollar
of Own Source Revenue: 1986

Special districts	$0.26
Cities	$0.15
Counties	$0.08
Townships	$0.08
School districts	$0.02

Source: Bollens, 1986:119.

is debt that does not require repayment of all principal and interest to be backed by local taxing power; instead, repayment is dependent upon successfully collected user fees.[25]) The debt outstanding was up 74% from just five years earlier, and nonguaranteed debt had increased by 95.3%.[26] The general obligation bonds (which constitute guaranteed debt) usually issued by cities require a referendum.[27] The revenue bonds (nonguaranteed debt) issued by special district governments, however, do not generally require a referendum. These revenue bonds have higher interest rates than do general obligation bonds.[28]

Two points are important here. First, the financial activities of even special districts involve huge amounts of money. Creating a special district means creating a major institution of public finance, an institution with the ability to tax, assess fees, and issue debt. Second, special districts provide different ways to finance local services than are available in municipal institutions. The main difference is special district reliance upon nonguaranteed debt, the issuance of which does not require local referendums.

Municipalities. Municipal finances are different in other respects from special district finances. Cities receive more money from state governments (20.2% of their general revenues) and less money from the federal government (8% of their general revenues) than do special districts; their total revenues from intergovernmental grants, however, have been about the same percentage of their general revenues as have been those for special districts.[29] Municipalities rely more heavily on property taxes (20.5% of municipal revenue) and sales taxes (12%) than do special districts.[30] Some municipal governments also levy taxes on businesses.[31]

The governments and their boundaries, then, define who does and does not contribute financially to the operation of local government. The kind of government created also demarcates the availability of debt, the character of local taxation, the extent to which citizens can participate in decisions about local finances, and the extent to which citizens can take advantage of money from the federal government for local projects.

In summary, the differences between these types of local government are significant because the governments have the institutional capacity to provide services, control huge amounts of money, and define the character of local political participation and accountability. In light of these differences, how can we explain why citizens have created cities and special districts, and how can we explain the preference for creating special districts in recent years? What does this tell us about the changing character of local politics in the United States?

The Logic of Local Government Formation

Traditional scholarship on the creation of special districts suggests that these districts are largely a technical financing maneuver by existing local governments that have hit taxing and debt limits and yet want to continue providing services.[32] In 1957, Bollens composed a list of reasons for the formation of special districts on the basis of his extensive study of these districts. He argued that they were formed because existing local governments were unsuitable, because people wanted independence, because existing governments wanted them, because it was expedient, and, finally, because it served some people's self-interest. The self-interested actors Bollens noted were equipment vendors, taxpayers, and people who want jobs.[33] Bollens' complete list has been repeated frequently in the years since he composed it.[34] Most recent work, however, focuses almost exclusively upon the technical financing maneuver explanation for these districts; this explanation has become accepted wisdom about why we have special districts.[35] To the extent that there is a traditional scholarship on municipal formation, the work has sometimes argued that the formation of cities is a natural consequence of population growth or of population movement;[36] that it is a consequence of a search for lower taxes;[37] that it is a consequence of racism;[38] or that it is a desire for a particular bundle of services.[39]

These are important, but incomplete, accounts. They are incomplete because they miss the fact that creating a new local government is a costly political act that often fails. Moreover, they miss the politics of creating these institutions, politics that mean that some people's values are institutionalized in local government and other people's values are not.[40]

Subsequent chapters explain these dynamics more fully; my goal in the remainder of this chapter is to sketch briefly the logic that underlies them.

The Problem: Forging Collective Action

People who want to form a new government face a collective action problem.[41] If a group of people is interested in forming a government for similar reasons (lower taxes or racial exclusion, for example), each person in the group would be better off if someone else took on the burden of forming the government. These individuals would still receive whatever benefits the new government had to offer, even if they themselves did not act to create the government. Thus, among citizens interested in forming a new government, the incentives to free-ride on the actions of others are high. As a consequence, creating a government is difficult.

Ultimately, I argue, the creations of these new governments are efforts to acquire access to the institutions that compose local governments— that is, access to the powers of local governments. State laws define these powers. State laws also define who can create a government to capture the institutional prize. This second set of laws specifies the solutions to the collective action problem of forming a new government. These laws specify the path people have to take to form a new government, and they specify how many people have to be involved. When the rules that define local governments are combined with the mechanisms necessary to solve the collective action problem of forming a new government to gain access to these institutions, many of the parameters of local government are set.

The Players: Who Can Solve the Collective Action Problem?

State governments specify the relevant solutions to the collective action problem because they make the rules for creating a new local government. They set up requirements that make it difficult to form a new local government. In many states, citizens must follow a set of formal procedures to form a new goverment—a set of procedures outlined in a general formation law. Depending on the type of government, there may be referendum requirements, population requirements, and area requirements. Some states—Georgia, for example—have an additional hurdle. Forming a new local government in these states requires a special act of the legislature.

The laws define the creation of a new local government as a collective action problem.[42] Moreover, when they specify requirements for the formation process, the laws specify the solutions to this collective action problem. In the United States today, states specify three primary solutions to the collective action problem of forming a new local government.[43]

The first solution is to obviate the collective action problem by *not* requiring petition signatures or referendum votes or a particular population size. In this instance, the collective action problem is solved by a small group.[44] This solution is prevalent in special district formation laws. Small groups (even as small as one person) should take advantage of this solution when they are interested in uncompromised access to the institutions of the local government (or, more specifically, the institutions— the powers—of the *special district*).

The second solution is an entrepreneurial one; individuals join in to satisfy the petition, referendum, or population requirements for local government formation when a very interested entrepreneur provides the start-up resources for organization.[45] This solution is most common for municipalities, where referendum, petition, and population requirements are prevalent. The entrepreneur needs three things: (1) abundant resources (so that the cost of the effort becomes *relatively* small), (2) interest in access to the powers of the new government, and (3) an ability to persuade enough citizens to support the referendum or sign the petition. Depending upon the nature of the collective action that the entrepreneur puts together, the entrepreneur's access to these institutions may or may not be exclusive.

The third solution to the collective action problem is the existence of an organized group that can be used for the purpose of creating a new local government.[46] The organizational problem has already been solved, and the indigenous organization can be retooled as the organizational base for the new collective action. This solution is more prevalent in efforts to create new cities than in efforts to form special districts, although there are examples in both.

The Prize: Who Wants What from Local Government?

The institutions of local government are the powers and capabilities of local government. States define whether municipalities can zone, how they can tax, the level of debt they can issue, and the kinds of services these governments provide. States also define the kinds and amounts of bonds special districts can issue, the kinds of services they can provide, and whether their politics are open to all residents or only to property owners. The federal government modifies these rules periodically with Supreme Court decisions on the constitutionality of certain rules and with legislation (such as the Voting Rights Act) that alters the ways in which the powers of local government can be used.

Clearly, the rules change over time and are not necessarily the same from one state to the next. For example, the powers of the city did not include zoning until 1916. Zoning permitted *local governments* to dictate more forcefully who lived where and who could be excluded from a city. After 1916, the creation of a new city could be an exclusionary effort, whereas between 1830 and 1916, cities were less able to homogenize local populations along class and racial lines. When the institutions change, citizens, not surprisingly, have new things to fight over.

What, more specifically, do citizens fight over today, and which forms of local government best satisfy their desires?

Citizens can gain access to *service provision* by forming either a city or a special district. Beginning sometime in this century and becoming quite pronounced with the local tax increases of the 1960s, cities became a significantly more expensive choice.[47] In more recent times, citizens have turned more and more to easier-to-form, easier-to-control special districts to gain access to desired new services.

The *tax-free, low-interest bond market* is similar to service provision. If one merely wants access to the ability to issue tax-free (low-interest) bonds, one would again turn to the potentially less costly, easier-to-form, and easier-to-control option of the special district.

Altering the taxation level is a clear reason to form a new city. Here the only option is a municipality, since municipalities do not overlap one another and since one would not be protected from high municipal taxes with a special district. Citizens seeking lower taxes can form new cities in order to keep their taxes low—particularly when they are faced with annexation efforts by older cities with higher taxes.

One might also create a new city in order to gain access to the *power to zone* and the concomitant *power to exclude* unwanted others. When the zoning is, for example, for large lot sizes or when it excludes apartment buildings, zoning can be used to exclude those with lower incomes who might want social services from the local government. It can also be used by whites wishing to exclude most African-Americans. In most instances, cities' power to zone can only be used to exclude those groups who have lower incomes than the group doing the excluding. Again, special districts do not zone, so a municipality is the only option.

Thus, the private values that individuals might want to institutionalize in *public* local governments are (1) low-tax sentiments, (2) preference for more publicly provided services or for the ability to use the bond market to provide those services, and (3) desire for exclusion.

The Result: Private Values in Public Institutions

Taken together, the players, prizes, rules, and obstacles in the formation of local governments begin to outline local politics in the United States. In particular, they point to those who have both *heightened interest* in gaining access to the powers of government and *abundant resources* to overcome the collective action problem as major players in local politics.

The most obvious and systematic entrepreneurs—with both abundant resources and heightened interest—for the low-tax case are businesses, which also want low taxes. The most obvious entrepreneurs for the second case—services—are developers who want government to build infrastructure to improve land to profit the developer. The most obvious entrepreneur in the last case is a homeowners' association whose interests complement those of the entrepreneur who wants low taxes. The only legal mechanism whites can use to exclude African-Americans is zoning, which would ultimately affect any person with a low income, not just African-Americans with low incomes. In practice, the two goals (keeping taxes low and excluding others) can be complementary even if the motivations are very different.

In the end, those who engage successfully in collective action embed their own private values in these public institutions of local government. Those individuals who work to create a new local government tend to be the people who have access to the institutions at least during the government's early stages.[48] Moreover, these founders create governments that persist in American politics and continue to structure those politics and define citizenship long after their creators are gone.

The evidence and discussions in the remainder of this work illuminate the role of businesses, economic motives, racial division, and mundane service desires in the structuring of local politics in America. They also provide insight into collective action problems. These formations are instances of very risky, costly collective action efforts. They often fail, particularly when they are not supported financially and organizationally by businesses, developers, and existing well-to-do organizations. Because it is the movements supported by these businesses, developers, and wealthy groups that succeed, if we looked solely at the outcomes, economic motives would appear to be the single cause of governmental formations. That would miss much of the story. It would miss the fact that often what enables these economic motives to succeed is the multiplicity of citizens' motives and the fact that businesses and developers take advantage of this multiplicity of motives and channel these motives in a way that redounds to the economic benefit of these businesses and developers. The citizens' motives are allowed to win through this channeling. The desire for lower taxes wins. The desire for new services wins. The desire for racial exclusion wins. And in some instances, it is the coincidence of entrepreneurial motives and these collective pressures that enables the collective action to succeed.

Conclusion

This is a brief introduction to the argument I will develop and support in the remainder of this work. In Chapter 2, I examine instances of efforts to create local governments from 1630 through the late twentieth century. These cases illustrate formation efforts and provide insight into the motivations that lead citizens, small groups, and entrepreneurs to create local governments; they begin to provide a sense of why some movements succeed and some fail. Chapter 3 places these cases of government creation within the context of the history of the definition and redefinition of the institutions of American local government. The evidence in this chapter is institutional history. This evidence points to why some motivations were prevalent at some times and not at others. It illuminates the changing character of the institutions of American local government and points to some of the sources of the changing significance of local governments and their boundaries and the changing content of local politics. In Chapter 4, I provide a closer examination of the formation of cities and special districts from 1950 through 1987. This chapter sets up the analyses discussed in Chapter 5. Chapter 5 looks more closely at citizens' efforts to form local governments from 1950 through 1987. This chapter builds upon Chapters 2 and 3 to clarify the changing significance of local politics and boundaries over these thirty-seven years and to sort out the effects of the motivations documented in Chapter 2. This chapter sorts out why citizens in some places at some times form governments, while at other times and in other places they do not. In addition, the chapter provides evidence concerning the specific connections between entrepreneurial activity and citizens' motivations in the formation of local governments. Chapter 6 concludes the work with a discussion of the findings and of the ways in which these findings inform our understanding of American politics and push us to focus upon the broader institutions of *government* as well as the narrower institutions of *governance*.

2

Particulars of Politics

This report is dedicated to the people of Levittown. If, after reading it, incorporation is their desire, may their efforts toward that
goal be spurred by pure motives; may their goal be achieved with
dignity; and may the monument they form be a brilliant example
of clean and rigidly honest government.
>   —Incorporation Study Committee of the
>   Levittown Civic Association,
>   Levittown, Pennsylvania, 1954[1]

TEN REASONS FOR INCORPORATION . . . REASON ONE: There will be
NO CITY PROPERTY TAX in the future city of East Los Angeles . . .
REASON SEVEN: Incorporation does not mean any higher taxes.
>   —Citizens' Committee to Incorporate
>   East Los Angeles, California, 1961[2]

The case studies in this chapter contribute an understanding of the details
of the successful collective actions that are the government formations.
As we will see, the constants of government formation are the particular
successful solutions to these collective action problems.

In different instances, the providers of the organization and resources
for the successful efforts are developers, shopping center owners, religious institutions, wealthy homeowners' associations, and manufacturers.
There are a range of reasons why these entrepreneurs and groups have
wanted governments. However, the two most ubiquitous groups and
entrepreneurs—developers and businesses—have wanted these governments for quite systematic and specific reasons. Developers have wanted
them because they improve land at little cost to the developer, and businesses have wanted them because young, business-created governments

can provide particularly congenial business climates with low taxes and friendly regulation. Because developers tend to act in the context of a small group, they very successfully tailor the institutions to their desires. Manufacturers, on the other hand, must act as entrepreneurs because they wish to create municipalities; they are thus more constrained in their ability to tailor-make the institutions. While they can channel citizens' desires, they also must at some point have citizens' signatures and citizens' votes to create the government (unlike the case of special districts).

Sometimes citizens want these governments because they provide mechanisms by which the citizens can select the other citizens of the government—inspections of potential residents in the 1600s and zoning powers in the 1900s. Through these mechanisms, citizens can be assured of low tax burdens at least for a time. In one era, white citizens interested in racial exclusion could employ these mechanisms to exclude African-Americans. In other eras, citizens have wanted these governments simply for the services they could provide. These case studies suggest that the common thread in successful formation efforts is business support for the effort. When business opposes the creation of a new government, even citizens who intensely want a new government fail to create one.

The Character of the Evidence

The evidence I present in this chapter consists of cases noted in studies of the formation of these institutions, in newspaper articles, and in scholarly discussions of other topics ranging from the separation of church and state to the ways in which individuals cope with local plant closings to the efforts of communities to deal with what residents perceive as witchcraft. These are not all of the case studies that exist; they are the ones I found after extensive searching.

The cases range from formations in the 1600s to formations in the 1980s. They range in depth. Often I reinterpret the data presented by the author of the case study, highlighting features of the case that the original author included but considered relatively unimportant. Generally, these features are the existence of entrepreneurs, but sometimes they are also interpretations of collective pressures. These cases undergird the quantitative analyses presented in Chapter 5. They provide the interesting details of politics and present portraits of individual formation efforts, of successful solutions to the collective action problem of government creation.

Special Districts

Citizens create special districts in order to acquire services. Small groups (or single individuals) form them to acquire services and access to eminent domain and, sometimes, to acquire lower taxes. These small groups—generally consisting of developers—dominate the politics of special district formation.

Services

Developers have wanted these districts for two reasons: to acquire access to the districts' power of eminent domain and to acquire access to their ability to fund infrastructure through the issuance of revenue bonds. Both of these powers reduce the risk and cost of development. In a sense, these special districts are unrestricted, publicly supported incentives for development.

Access to special districts' power of eminent domain appeared first. In the 1800s, it was "common legislative practice . . . [to pass] special acts vacating streets at the behest of private persons in interest and of opening and improving streets at the behest of land speculators and contractors."[3] These acts often entailed the creation of special districts.[4] In some instances, these early districts provided mechanisms to achieve development *and* to segment costs such that only the "interested" paid for improvements.[5]

Later, in 1935, the National Association of Real Estate Boards (NAREB) proposed Neighborhood Protection and Improvement Districts to the Roosevelt administration; NAREB's proposal was not successful. The point of these districts would have been to simplify land assembly. These districts would, NAREB believed, make it easier to revitalize urban neighborhoods and business districts. The district officials would have the power to carry out revitalization plans because they would have the power to condemn buildings that stood in the way of redevelopment *and* they could levy taxes to fund redevelopment.[6]

More recent (1990) efforts are reminiscent of these early attempts to create districts.[7] In particular, businesses and developers wanted to form a special district in Detroit that would have the power to raze 740 acres to create a district that would foster (as the developers and businesses who drafted the plan note) "practical family values . . . in an atmosphere free of drugs, prostitution, pornography, gambling and other criminal activity."[8] Clearly, too, the district would make development more profitable in the process. Groups have made similar proposals in Houston.[9]

Developers have also wanted special districts because they can fund the provision of infrastructure to improve land and make it valuable for development. These governments are able to lower the costs and the risks of development.

The Urban Land Institute points out that, at least in the Institute's opinion, special districts' "primary purpose" is to finance the start-up costs of development through public taxes rather than through private, developer-provided funds. In Texas, for example, the predominant form of special district, the Municipal Utility District, is formed by the request of a developer and is governed by officials recommended by the developer.[10] While developers must hold a vote on district creation among the new district's residents, since there are generally few if any residents, this is not a significant hurdle for the developers. Developers simply move a few people into the district and set them up in mobile homes or new homes that they sell at cost to these new residents. In turn, residents agree to support the formation of the new district.[11] Clearly, these developers understand how to use selective incentives to their advantage, and in some instances they have the resources to provide these incentives. A *Sacramento Business Journal* article supports this picture; the article notes that a particular type of district "requires a two-thirds vote of the property owners within the proposed district. Thus, *it is most practical when raw land is involved and only the developers vote.*"[12] In the end, developers get what they want. They maintain control over the district for the first few years.[13]

There are many other examples of developers' efforts to create special districts to fund infrastructure. Developers of a resort near Naples, Florida, formed a special district in 1974.[14] The developers felt that Naples would not be able to provide the development with enough water, and Naples' wastewater treatment facilities, they believed, would not be adequate for the planned resort. The developers used the district to fund the installation of basic services for their new resort—water and sewerage, lighting, and drainage.[15] Developers created another district, the North Pleasanton Improvement District of Pleasanton, California, in the early 1980s.[16] This district funds road improvements that in the past were largely funded by developers.

Developers in Washington State in 1987 supported the transportation districts created by the state legislature with House Bill 396. These districts allowed developers to avoid paying for highway improvement. Ted Knapp, the director of real estate operations for Upland Industries, said, "The private sector is increasingly being asked to pick up the tab for a major share of these [highway improvement] costs." In particular, Knapp worried about the alternative to special districts, impact fees, which he argued caused developers to avoid some sites. Special districts solved the developers' problems.[17]

Developers were interested in these districts because the districts could generate public funds for development <u>and</u> because they would give developers almost complete control over how these funds would be spent. Developers have considered these districts as alternatives to annexation since at least the 1950s.[18] Recently, developers have come to see these districts as a way around impact fees.

Sometimes other businesses join developers to form a special district, as they did in Cobb County, Georgia, in 1985. The businesses and developers were concerned about road improvements; they banded together to form a special district to tax themselves and other property owners in the area. Phil Sanders, president of the Cobb County Chamber of Commerce, argued that "Businessmen realize that local government couldn't pay for all the necessary infrastructure improvements by itself. Someone had to help." The Cobb County Chamber lobbied the state legislature to revise the state constitution to permit businesses to set up special tax districts.[19] Businesses proposed similar districts in Tysons Corner, Virginia.[20]

Again, this business interest in the capabilities of special districts is not recent. At the turn of the twentieth century, business leaders in the lower Mississippi Valley were also interested in forming special districts, this time to reclaim swamplands along the Mississippi River for development.[21]

The formation of the Steel Valley Authority in the Monongahela River Valley provides an example of a different source of the organization and resources that developers usually provide. In this case, citizens wanted the special district because it could provide funding for projects *and* because it could enforce cooperation.[22]

The source of resources to sustain the movement was the Tri-State Conference on Steel, a coalition of local government officials, labor, clergy, and workers.[23] In the wake of the 1984 closing of the Duquesne mill, the members of the Tri-State Conference devised the plan for the Authority; they wanted intergovernmental cooperation to rebuild the steel industry.[24] They wanted an intermunicipal organization that could develop a systematic plan for dealing with plant closings.[25] This Authority would buy a closing plant and operate it, or it would try to find another company to buy the plant. The process of creating the Authority took several years; the Tri-State Conference on Steel sustained the effort to create the authority.

Special districts can also accomplish limited forms of job creation; many districts (59% in 1987) have employees, and some districts require specialized equipment.[26] Potential employees and equipment vendors have an interest in forming special districts to gain jobs and sales. Interview data from a study of special districts in Arizona point to fire service and equipment firms' role in creating fire districts.[27] These firms encourage interest in a district, provide information about how to form a district, and pay some of the expenses of forming the district. The companies are rewarded; they get new service contracts and more equipment sales from their efforts.[28]

State actions have provided the opportunity for other kinds of service desires—services that still take advantage of the capacity of special districts to fund projects—to translate into new special district governments. In the 1890s, for example, the State of Massachusetts imposed a series of regional special district governments upon the Boston metropolitan area to deal with metropolitanwide problems at a time when there was no consensus on issues of annexation.[29] Thus, the state formed the Metropolitan Sewer Commission in 1889, the Metropolitan Park District in 1893, and the Metropolitan Water District in 1895 in order to force metropolitanwide cooperation on problems that no smaller area could solve on its own.

Water politics in Southern California from the 1920s through the 1940s provide a related example.[30] Existing organizations—this time local governments—sustained the creation of a major water district in Southern California. These local governments wanted the district, first, because it could float bonds and, second, because it could ensure cooperation in the provision of water for Southern California. By establishing a district, the governments were able to ensure that there would be no free riders in Southern California water politics. Access to the water required being a member of the district; being a member of the district required supporting the district's activities financially.

Los Angeles in the 1920s was working to create a long-term water supply for the development of Southern California; Los Angeles' officials wanted to bring water from the Colorado River to Southern California to accomplish this. Los Angeles was the only governmental unit in the area with the funds necessary to undertake such a project, since the price tag was $220 million. The Chief Engineer and General Manager of Los Angeles, William Mulholland, devised the idea for this aqueduct in 1921. In 1923 he asked for funds from the Board of Public Service Commissioners to begin a feasibility survey. In order for the project to be successful, a number of the communities in Southern California had to participate. Initially, no one had a clear sense of how this could be accomplished. Finally, in 1924, the *Los Angeles Times*, in an editorial, suggested a cooperative agreement among the four counties involved. An organization composed of local government officials revised this proposal to one for the formation of a water district. The district would issue bonds for building the aqueduct. The California state legislature eventually passed general enabling legislation for metropolitan water districts. In 1928, local governments in Southern California formed the Metropolitan Water District of Southern California.[31]

Other cases of southwestern water politics suggest different motivations for creating these districts.[32] These other case studies point to the huge developmental impact of water and irrigation districts. Not surprisingly, their prime sponsors are developers and industrialists. The commonalities with the other districts, again, are the interest of developers and the fact that they can float bonds.

One particularly striking example of this type of politics is the effort to form the Rancho del Rio Grande Conservancy District.[33] The plan was for this district to operate the Indian Camp Dam, a federally funded water project. When the dam was proposed in 1971, the population of the area seemed to support the idea of building it. The fact that the dam was only half of the package, that the rest of the package was a conservancy district, was not yet apparent.

In the summer of 1971, by the time the state and local authorities had rounded up a group of indigenous people to petition for the conservancy and the dam, there had developed firm opposition to the project—based almost entirely in the Chicano small farmers, who were allegedly to benefit from the district, and who were caught at the time in the heart of a severe drought.

On the other hand, the businessmen of Taos, the real estate agents, lawyers, bankers, and tourist agents—in short, those who seemed to have nothing to do with small subsistence farming and the water involved therewith were most avidly pushing the district and the dam.[34]

The indigenous population lived on small subsistence farms; the residents were poor, with an annual per capita income of $1,300. They believed they could not afford the cost of the dam and, in particular, the cost of the district.

The special assistant to the State Engineer, Paul Bloom, said:

> This project is an attempt on the part of the government to reverse the flight of the farmer from the land to the barrios of Albuquerque or Los Angeles. This is a project that is reserved for marginal farmers and is aimed at keeping them from boarding up their homes and leaving.
>
> In support of himself, Bloom referred to another New Mexico irrigation project, the Elephant Butte Dam: "Ask people near Elephant Butte," he said, "and they will tell you the dam was a godsend that has made acequia farming into a prosperous business."[35]

However, the Elephant Butte Dam and Conservancy District had actually raised the costs of subsistence farming significantly. According to a 1936 study of resource dependency in the Rio Grande Watershed, the Elephant Butte water project made "bankruptcy and the loss of farms" "a constant threat. . . . Many of the original Spanish-American farmers, in the process of commercialization, were removed from their land through foreclosure."[36]

In the Middle Rio Grande Conservancy District, which bankers and land entrepreneurs created in the mid 1920s, taxes increased dramatically in order to pay off the $9,500,000 in bonds. In ten years, 70% of the assessments were delinquent and 8,000 people lost title to their land, according to one account.[37]

The district serving the Indian Camp Dam was formed, over the objections of the Latino and Native American populations. The New Mexico Supreme Court later declared the district's formation unconstitutional.[38]

Business Climates and Taxes

Some district creations center on the issues of business climate and taxes. Here the reasons the districts are so useful are that they can fund infrastructure creation and improvement and they have geographic boundaries—defining some people into the government and some out.

A particularly interesting special district formation effort created the Reedy Creek Improvement District in Orlando, Florida, in 1967. This district *is* Walt Disney World. In the negotiations between Walt Disney and the state of Florida, Disney's *first* legal request was for the creation of the Reedy Creek Drainage District.[39] The district

> would have the power to regulate land use, provide police and fire
> service, build roads, lay sewer lines, construct waste-treatment plants,
> carry out flood control projects—even to build an airport. In addition,
> it would be empowered to issue bonds and to levy a property tax on
> its landowner, Disney.[40]

The district meant that surrounding local governments could not impose growth controls *or* impact fees for building and maintenance of the roads leading to Disney World.[41] A similar case is a Houston special district that governs an area wholly owned by a subsidiary of Humble Oil.[42]

These cases point to several reasons why individuals (generally not a large group of citizens and, far more frequently, almost solely a developer or business) have created special districts. Their motivations rest largely upon the capacity of special districts to issue revenue bonds, although these districts' power of eminent domain, their ability to stabilize cooperation, the fact that they sometimes have employees and need specialized equipment, and the necessity to have a geographical base are also important. These efforts succeed when there is a source of organization and money to sustain the formation effort. The most systematically present source of sustenance is a small group composed of a single developer with clear motives for forming a special district. However, there are other sources—such as existing organizations—that can provide this sustenance.

These formations are not simply technical financing maneuvers. They are instead implicit decisions about who pays for development in the United States. By and large, they have been efforts by developers to use public financing for development. States clearly have encouraged this by allowing developers to create these governments in the first place.

States and citizens underwrite development with these districts in much the same way that states and municipalities issued franchises to businesses to speed development in an earlier era.

Municipalities

Both cities and special districts can fund services. The differences between the two forms of government, however, are crucial. Municipalities generally must have referendums when they issue bonds, municipalities have a more visible and participatory politics, municipalities can zone, and a higher percentage of municipalities can assess taxes than can special districts.

The two kinds of governments are very different in the eyes of potential political entrepreneurs and from the perspective of other sources of organization and financing for collective action. Cities can maintain more exclusive control over taxation, service levels, and the character of the population. While cities are more powerful bundles of institutions, creating a city is more difficult than creating a special district; a city is also more difficult to control once created. Special districts, on the other hand, can provide infrastructure in a manner that provides a potential windfall for a developer, and these districts institute a less visible politics in which to make decisions about this infrastructure. Moreover, the formation of these districts does not require many citizens. In the end, the developer's values are institutionalized without much compromise.

Instances of municipal formation efforts are rarely the small-group efforts that dominate special district formations. Instead, because states require new cities to have a certain number of citizens, the efforts are largely entrepreneurial. Sometimes, of course, they rely upon existing resource-rich organizations. In the end, like the citizens who form special districts, the citizens who create cities are most successful when they take advantage of the developmental potential of these governments.

Services

Citizens form municipalities sometimes because they simply cannot acquire the services they want from existing governments.[43] Cities can provide these public services because they can tax and issue bonds.

An early example of this kind of service incorporation is the battle to incorporate Wilkinsburg, Pennsylvania, a rapidly growing, fashionable suburb of Pittsburgh, in 1886. The effort ended up as a fight between two coalitions: the pro-bathtub coalition and the anti-bathtub coalition. A spokesperson for the anti-bathtub group argued that the incorporation effort

> was started by a lot of those city "fellers" who want to introduce new-fangled city improvements at the taxpayers' expense—such things as sewers, paved streets, public water supply, and bath tubs—"fellers" who are too lazy to bring a tub up from the cellar on a Saturday night.[44]

The pro-bathtub group won.

Developers proved important in service incorporations in the 1800s when expanses of the West opened up for settlement; they used new cities much like the developers noted above used special districts. The new cities made speculators' land valuable. Western legislatures received so many requests from speculators to incorporate new towns that these legislatures were the first to enact general incorporation procedures. As Teaford argues,

> one of the first steps in the progression to imperial glory [on the part of the town] was incorporation, and consequently swarms of developers badgered their state legislators for municipal charters.[45]

The first general incorporation law passed in the Louisiana Territory in 1808. Nine years later, similar legislation passed in Indiana and Ohio. In 1825, Missouri passed a general incorporation law. Nine states soon followed.[46]

One example of the efforts of these early developers is the founding of Grand Junction, Colorado. In 1881, speculators arrived in what they were to call Grand Junction. In 1882, settlers were officially allowed into western Colorado. To ensure that the town they wished to build would have citizens, the speculators pressed settlers to incorporate the town of Grand Junction. The thirty-three voters complied.[47] The speculators set up all of the ingredients of the town; they built the post office, started a newspaper, imported residents, and set up the meeting to propose incorporation. The developers paid the first mayor's way to the federal land office in Leadville to file for incorporation.[48] As Jackson and Schultz argue, in nineteenth-century America, real-estate speculators spent much of their time building cities.[49]

Hamilton's work on the creation of African-American towns in the late 1800s underlines the role of developer speculation in town creation. Hamilton studied the creation of Allensworth, California; Nicodemus, Kansas; Mound Bayou, Mississippi; Boley, Oklahoma; and Langston City, Oklahoma. His work argues that African-American and white speculators saw African-Americans as basically a new market for towns after Emancipation. The speculators seeking to create African-American towns advertised their new cities widely. And in many instances they were able to blend the appeal of the new town with a Black Nationalist theme. In Hamilton's words,

> The speculators who founded the five towns . . . only inadvertently made race and the desire to escape white hostility a part of their promotional effort. Conditions of their time encouraged black-town developers to embrace racial uplift ideas, but economic motives rather than racism led to the inception of Trans-Appalachian black towns.[50]

This notion that the form of the city could be used to increase land values was current long before the speculators gained access to the Western plains. Lockridge argues that town formation in the early 1700s in New England was an attempt on the part of outlivers to increase the value of their land. The outlivers petitioned to secede from the existing town and form their own government. They claimed that it was a matter of convenience; but Lockridge argues that simply by obtaining their own church and town meetings, they enticed new settlers and increased the demand for the surrounding property.[51] In addition to increasing the value of their land, the formations, Lockridge argues, increased the consensus on such issues as meeting locations.[52] An important example of one such effort is Salem, Massachusetts. Scholars have argued that part of the reason for the Salem witch trials was that Salem Town refused to let Salem Village secede to form an independent town. The residents of Salem Village faced land constraints and consequent decreasing income; the residents of Salem Town had access to other forms of income because the male residents there were largely merchants. Salem Village repeatedly petitioned for its own government; just as repeatedly, Salem Town refused. The Salem witch trial accusers were from Salem Village; the accused were from Salem Town.[53]

Even early service incorporations often required entrepreneurial support from businesses or developers in order to succeed.[54] Binford notes the role of what he calls "young entrepreneurs" in the nineteenth-century formation of Somerville and Cambridge, Massachusetts.[55] Somerville broke from the Charlestown peninsula to form a separate town, and the existing town of Cambridge incorporated as a city (the fourth to do so in Massachusetts). Efforts to create Somerville and to incorporate Cambridge without entrepreneurial support failed. With entrepreneurs—businesspersons and real estate dealers—to sustain the movement, the creation efforts succeeded.

More recent examples of the importance of entrepreneurs in service incorporation efforts are attempts to incorporate East Los Angeles, California, which have generally been attempts to acquire more services and create more of a Latino community identity. These attempts seem to be genuine grass-roots movements; however, due to lack of entrepreneurial support and to what is often strong opposition, these movements have failed repeatedly. Beginning in 1932, business interests opposed the incorporation of East Los Angeles. Only in 1961 did a business interest support the incorporation effort—the Safeway Corporation (along with the county fire department). But another group of businesses opposed the incorporation attempt in 1961.[56]

Other service incorporations are Hyde Park, Massachusetts, in 1868; South Omaha, Nebraska, in 1886; Elyria, Colorado, in 1890; West Cleveland, Ohio, in 1871; Norwood, Ohio, in the late 1800s; Grandview Heights, Ohio, in 1906; Whitefish Bay, Wisconsin, in 1892; Azusa, California, in 1898; Brook Park, Ohio, in 1914; and Roseland, New Jersey, in 1908.[57]

Race and Class Divisions

Cities are also capable of dividing races and classes. Early cities and towns had laws enabling inspection of potential residents. More recently, cities have gained the power to zone. As a consequence of these powers of resident inspection and zoning, exclusionary zeal in various forms has been a part of American local institutions from their beginning.[58]

The earliest tradition is the establishment of towns that create economic homogeneity—mainly for the well-to-do. In the seventeenth century this process was aided by English merchants who planned the colonization of New England.[59] The resulting communities are exemplified by the founding of Watertown, Massachusetts, in the late 1630s: "Everyone hoped that there would be no poor, and Watertown had made special provisions to exclude them."[60] To that end, they established that "anyone who 'may prove chargeable to the town' could be ordered to leave."[61] The town's creators wanted to maintain social order and avoid the high taxes that they had faced in England—high taxes that would result from the local government's obligation to support poor residents.[62] The founders of Sudbury, Massachusetts, shared the sentiments of the Watertown founders.[63] The founders of Marlborough, Massachusetts, decreed that "No man was allowed to join the community unless he passed their inspection."[64] A local constable in seventeenth-century Virginia included among his list of fees a fee "For removing any person suspected to become chargeable to the parish; to be paid by the parish for every mile going and returning . . . 2 [pounds of tobacco]."[65]

Whites have tried to use cities to exclude African-Americans. One racially motivated attempt that failed occurred in Atlanta in 1887. Some members of Atlanta's white elite devised plans to create a separate city for African-Americans adjoining Atlanta's south side. The white elite planned to force all of Atlanta's African-American residents to move to the new city in order to create an all-white Atlanta.[66]

In a more recent, successful effort, church groups in St. Louis decided to purchase twelve acres of land in Black Jack, Missouri, an unincorporated section of St. Louis County, in 1969.[67] The land was zoned for multiple-family dwellings. The groups planned to build racially integrated, moderate-income housing on the site.[68] Almost immediately, the white residents of the area employed their Black Jack Improvement Association to distribute circulars and hold meetings to develop opposition to building integrated housing in the area. They traveled to Washington, D.C., to present petitions to the Department of Housing and Urban Development (HUD) to stop the public housing development. The trip was unsuccessful; HUD agreed to finance the project. Within two weeks, the white residents petitioned the St. Louis County Council to incorporate the area. They succeeded. Immediately upon forming the municipality, they zoned apartments—including publicly funded ones—out of the city.[69] The Nixon Justice Department filed an action against Black Jack in June 1971, arguing that the "rezoning was accomplished to exclude blacks from moving into Black Jack."[70]

A more recent (1991) effort centered on religious rather than racial exclusion. This time citizens used the zoning powers acquired through incorporation to exclude small synagogues in homes. By so doing, the residents of the newly incorporated Airmont, New York, were able to exclude Orthodox Jews who could not travel by car on the Sabbath.[71]

One variant of this argument for economic or racial exclusion is the notion that the formation of new municipalities is the result of a desire for local control.[72] This argument has two incarnations. One version is exclusionary. Jackson quotes a suburban Chicago editorial from 1907:

> The real issue is not taxes, nor water, nor street cars—it is a much greater question than either. It is the moral control of our village. . . . *Under local government we can absolutely control every objectionable thing that may try to enter our limits*—but once annexed we are at the mercy of city hall.[73]

The other version is an effort to bring government closer to the people. One example of this second form of local control is the series of attempts to create Mandela, Massachusetts. Boston residents tried twice to secede from Boston to form Mandela—once in 1986 and once in 1988. Rep. Byron Rushing, a supporter of the movement, argued that

> blacks cannot expect government to respond adequately to their needs until they are in the majority . . . and for Boston's blacks—who now comprise less than 30 percent of the population—that requires more black people "or different boundaries. . . . And it's simpler to draw lines on a map."[74]

The proponents of the new municipality planned to institute new taxes on commercial property and on developers' profits.[75] In 1986, downtown business interests were willing to provide $17,000 to fund the opposition to incorporation/secession.[76]

Incorporations have been spurred by efforts to homogenize politics for other reasons. A number of cities incorporated in order to ban alcohol: Pasadena, California, in the 1880s; South Pasadena, California, in 1888; Monrovia, California, in 1887; and Oak Park, Illinois, in 1902. Some cities incorporated for exactly the opposite reason, to maintain saloons: Madison, Illinois, in 1891, and Vernon, California, in 1905. There were also incorporations to maintain racetracks: Arcadia, California, in 1903, and North Randall, Ohio, in 1908.[77]

Taxes

Miller, in one of the strongest scholarly works yet written on incorporation, argues that incorporation is a response to citizens' fears of annexation and consequent higher taxes.[78] Clearly, citizens have created cities for other reasons. Nevertheless, in the Lakewood Plan cities in Los

Angeles County, California, that Miller studied, taxes dominate.[79] These Lakewood Plan cities were modeled on the plan to incorporate Lakewood, California; these new cities contracted with the county for most services, instead of providing the services themselves.

In the formation of Commerce, California, one of these Lakewood Plan cities, industries and homeowners wanted to use the new city as a mechanism for tax limitation.

> Local industry supplied the money to organize the incorporation; it hired the public relations firm that ran the incorporation election; and it financed the filing of incorporation papers and the mapping of incorporation boundaries.[80]

After incorporation, the local Industry Council proposed a slate of Anglo Republicans in the new city's first elections. The slate won, despite the fact that the population of Commerce was 60% Latino, 90+% Democratic, and mostly working class.[81]

Industries wanted to wall themselves off from the taxes necessary to support residential and social services when they incorporated the city of Industry, California.

> The incorporation petition was drawn to include virtually no residents, but as much of the prime industrial land along the railroads as possible. The boundaries were so neatly drawn, in fact, that with all its six square miles of land, the area had less than the requisite 500 inhabitants. Consequently, the proposal was drawn to include the 169 patients and 31 employees of a mental sanitarium, making the total population 629. The signatures of the incorporation petition included signatures representing realty firms and the two railroads. Over 50 percent of the land was owned by absentee landlords. . . . No residential building has been allowed there since incorporation.[82]

The city does not publish a budget, and the city council does not have a published agenda.[83] Nor does the city have an official spokesperson. Politics is quiet. The fact that cities can zone and the fact that cities have geographical boundaries make the cities useful for these businesses.

In the case of Lakewood, California, the leaders of the incorporation effort were a young attorney and a developer who was afraid that Long Beach was going to annex land containing his shopping center and increase taxes.[84] In fact, it was the developer and the attorney who channeled the original residential *support* for annexation into a movement for the incorporation of the wealthy suburb of Lakewood.[85] Ben Weingart, the developer, and John Todd, the attorney, decided that the way to fight the piecemeal annexation strategy was to obtain the signatures of property owners representing 50 percent of the land in each annexation increment. These signatures would automatically stop an annexation attempt, even if the property owners represented a small proportion of the population. This property owner protest, as it was called, would make it unnecessary to run election campaigns for each of the multiple increments.[86]

Weingart and Todd succeeded in quashing most of the annexation efforts. However, in 1952, Long Beach reached an agreement with Douglas Aircraft Corporation that included the annexation of the Douglas plant to Long Beach in exchange for expanding runways. South Lakewood was eventually annexed to Long Beach.

At this point, there was only one way that Weingart could prevent the annexation of his shopping center to the city of Long Beach: He proposed incorporation. Local taxpayers, though, continued to oppose it.[87] In 1953, businesspersons sponsored a study of the possibility of creating a contract city, a city that would contract with the county for services. By 1954, the businesses, Weingart, and Todd, "having carefully developed public sentiment for incorporation," succeeded in the last leg of the incorporation campaign.[88]

The developers and businesses were thus able to channel what was in fact anti-incorporation, pro-annexation sentiment into support for the formation of Lakewood, California. Without the developers and businesses, incorporation would not have even been suggested.[89]

Miller also describes the case of the incorporation of Signal Hill, California, which Long Beach attempted to annex in the early 1920s. Long Beach failed. During the annexation effort, a large oil field was discovered in the area to be annexed. The oil companies incorporated Signal Hill to stop Long Beach's attempts to annex it.[90]

Fleischmann argues that avoidance of high taxes is the reason for some incorporations around Milwaukee.[91] In 1985, proponents of the incorporation of Tortolita, Arizona, a community near Tucson, were worried about annexation as well.[92]

This theme is apparent in another (also failed) effort to form Levittown, Pennsylvania. The initial report of the Incorporation Study Committee of the Levittown Civic Association pointedly notes that the citizens of the new city would not be paying higher taxes. Moreover, the report mentions problems with a potential annexation by Middletown.[93]

Even for towns not founded explicitly by merchants or industrialists—towns in the Southwest that were founded mainly to increase the influence of the Spanish government—taxation levels were considered an important way to attract potential town founders. As Cruz notes, "Two of the most persuasive arguments promoting the Rio Grande colonies concerned the chance to acquire free land and tax exemptions for settlers signing up for the first entrada."[94] These new towns often had laws, such as the one passed in San Antonio in 1745, "commanding all bachelors, ruffians, and others . . . without any work . . . to look, within a period of one week for masters whom they may serve . . . or . . . depart from this villa."[95] Like the examples from the same era in New England, this worry was twofold. In part, it was a worry about social order. In part, it was a worry about taxation.

Entrepreneurs were important in efforts to form cities to acquire tax limitation and prevent annexation, as they were with some efforts to create cities to provide services. Hoch argues that *successful* incorporation attempts in Los Angeles County were initiated by the owners of industrial as opposed to residential land who were advantaged by the incorporation process.[96] Fleischmann notes:

> Boundary changes also allow firms to reduce operating expenses by avoiding taxes or regulation and by shifting development costs. Patrick Cuhady, for example, "skipped town" to avoid Milwaukee's proposed controls on meat packing and colonized an area south of the city which later incorporated. . . . Standard Oil employed a similar strategy in northern Indiana to sidestep taxation and air pollution regulation by Chicago.[97]

Sometimes other regulatory aspects of business climates are the impetus for city formation. There are two notable cases. First, William Penn granted a charter for Philadelphia in order to achieve "the better Regulation of Trade therein." In 1701, he chartered Chester for the same reason.[98] Later, industrialists in Pennsylvania employed municipal incorporation in order to create a friendly business climate. The industrialists who incorporated Scranton, Pennsylvania, used the new city to expand their businesses.[99]

Teaford points to a number of business- and tax-related incorporations around the turn of the twentieth century. Four cities incorporated for tax reasons: South Evanston, Illinois, in 1873; Brooklyn Heights, Ohio, in 1903; Whiting, Indiana, in 1894; and Munhall, Pennsylvania, in 1901. Two cities incorporated because businesses wished to avoid unfriendly regulation: Cuhady, Wisconsin, in 1892, and National City, Illinois, in 1906.[100] Standard Oil created Whiting, and Carnegie Steel incorporated Munhall.[101]

Other Sources of Organization and Resources

The organization and resources for municipal incorporation do not have to come from manufacturers, although manufacturers—at least in the twentieth century—have the most systematic reason for supporting a municipal incorporation movement. Miller points out, for example, that developers, utility companies, firefighters, and public relations consultants all play a role in creating cities.[102]

In one instance, a powerful religious organization succeeded in incorporating the city of Rajneeshpuram in Wasco County, Oregon.

> In 1981, the Indian guru Bhagwan Shree Rajneesh and his followers purchased a 64,229 acre parcel of land in rural Wasco County, Oregon. Thereafter, Bhagwan Shree Rajneesh and his followers, "Rajneeshees," took the necessary steps to incorporate over 2,000 acres of the parcel, now known as Rancho Rajneesh, as a municipality. On November 4, 1981, the Wasco County Court ordered that an incorporation election be held. The election was held on May 18, 1982, and the incorporation was approved by a unanimous vote of the 154 electors. On May 26, 1982, the Wasco County Court issued a Proclamation of Incorporation in which the city of Rajneeshpuram ("Rajneeshpuram" or the "City") was recognized as a putative municipal corporation under Oregon state law.[103]

The new city was notable in that its only public land consisted of one public road—formerly Road 305, renamed Sufi Road. The rest of the land was owned by a Rajneesh corporation, which controlled access to the property and by and large prohibited visitors from entering with its "peace force." Under Oregon's revenue-sharing formula, Rajneeshpuram received $10,484.86 in state funds in 1983.[104] The idea was to create a spiritual mecca. The city itself would provide the basic services to Rajneeshees.[105] The Rajneeshees planned to attract at least 100,000 of the 300,000 followers of the Bhagwan Shree Rajneesh to the city. Oregon state officials worried that this would make Rajneeshpuram the second largest city in Oregon. An Oregon federal court eventually declared the city unconstitutional as a violation of the separation of church and state.[106]

In addition to alternative forms of organization, an abundance of individual resources can also enable an incorporation movement to succeed. There are several California examples of incorporation movements by neighborhoods composed of wealthy individuals. Residents wanted cities in order to preserve the character and concomitant zoning of these wealthy enclaves (for example, these new municipalities allowed only certain shades of white paint).[107] Because the residents themselves had the resources to carry the movement, they did not need the support of manufacturers and other large organizations. The results were cities such as Rolling Hills Estates and Rolling Hills, California. Other examples of this form of incorporation are Woodruff Place, Indiana, in 1876; University City, Missouri, in 1902; and Lake Forest, Riverside, and Kenilworth, Illinois, around 1900.[108]

These examples of municipal incorporation movements point to the range of uses people have found for the form of the municipality. They have wanted these cities to provide them with services, low taxes, and exclusionary politics. By and large, citizens who have wanted cities in order to achieve these goals have succeeded only when they have had the active support of an organization with the resources to sustain the collective action. The most systematic sources of these organizational and financial resources have been interested businesses. Of course, the process sometimes has worked in the opposite direction. Businesses have wanted new cities and have channeled citizens' preferences to that end. This second form of the process has rarely failed. The consequence is that, in most instances of municipal incorporation, the values of citizens and the values of entrepreneurs are institutionalized in local politics.

Businesses expect to control these new governments. Waste argues, after studying several California incorporations, that those few individuals who work actively for incorporation tend to be the members of the first city council. Those who are active in the anti-incorporation movement lose when they run for a position on the first city council.[109] Businesses, then, can get what they want, at least in the first few years.

Conclusion

Citizens have wanted new special districts and new cities to provide services, to make their politics homogeneous, and to reduce their taxes. And, by and large, they have been able to acquire these governments when businesses and developers have enabled them to do so. When business has opposed or has been uninvolved, the citizens have often been unable to create or sustain the organization necessary to sustain a movement; and even when they could, the movements were not successful. Of course, there are exceptions to this pattern, times when citizens could overcome obstacles and create or rely upon alternative forms of organization to achieve the creation of a local government. Businesses and developers were simply more available and more interested than were many of the alternatives.

This set of cases of efforts to form governments is the first piece of evidence for my argument. In the next chapter, I build upon these cases to create a narrative of the institutional history of cities and special districts. In Chapter 5, I present results from an analysis of government formations over three and a half decades and 200 counties in the United States, evidence that speaks to the extent to which my argument can be generalized and that more clearly sorts out the *effects* of motives—and not just the *existence* of those motives—than can be accomplished by case studies.

3

Making Sense of the History

Oh, it was fun starting and running a city in those days!
—JAMES E. COOLEY, 1925[1]

Be it enacted by the authority aforesaid, That at any time after
the directors of the said society shall have made choice of a suit-
able place for the principal seat of their said manufactories . . . if
agreeable to the inhabitants of the said district, that the said inhabitants should be and become a body politic and corporate . . . by
the name and title of the Corporation of the Town of Paterson.
—STATE OF NEW JERSEY, 1791[2]

This chapter grounds the cases presented in Chapter 2 more firmly in
their historical context and constructs a history of the governments
themselves. In so doing, it places the institutions more starkly in relief
and points to the ways in which the successful solutions to the collective action problems of the governments' creation have changed (inten-
tentionally and unintentionally) over time.

Enterprising judges, technological developments, social movements,
developers, manufacturers, the Supreme Court, and state legislators have
continually redefined these governments, giving them more and less
autonomy, altering the kinds of services they can provide, and expanding their police powers. With these alterations, the possible successful
solutions to the collective action problem of creating a new government
have changed. As a consequence, the values institutionalized in American local governments have also changed.

Throughout, these governments have been more than administrative
divisions of the state. It is the ways in which they have been more than
administrative divisions—their autonomy, their power to define citizenship, their ability to float bonds, their power of eminent domain—that

have made them the focus of citizen, entrepreneurial, and group efforts to alter the structure of American local government over these 350 years.

Early U.S. Formations

In the United States, if the case studies noted in Chapter 2 are any guide, citizens established the earliest towns to increase the value of land, to exclude the poor and maintain social order, and to "settle Manufactures."[3] English authorities were particularly concerned that settlers "plant towns." In the 1660s, the proprietors of South Carolina told their colonists: "You and your council . . . are to choose some fitting place whereon to build a fort under the protection of which is to be your first town. . . . You are to order the people to plant towns."[4]

These early towns had only limited autonomy. However, gaining access to the powers that they did have was a crucial motivation for the creation of these towns.[5] The towns could administer a few important services, such as inspecting fences, roads, and grain. They could make land more valuable just by existing. Importantly for their potential creators, they could also enforce settlement laws and laws regarding who counted as an inhabitant. If potential new residents passed inspection by current residents and had sufficient documentation, they might not be "warned out." In 1741, for example, the Delaware Assembly passed a law for "the prevention of straggling and indigent persons from coming into and being chargeable to the inhabitants." The statute authorized local overseers of the poor to "make diligent inspection and inquiry . . . after all vagrant, poor and impotent persons . . . coming to settle or otherwise."[6] In North Carolina, a similar act began: "Whereas diverse idle and disorderly persons . . . frequently stroll from one county to another."[7] In Connecticut towns around the turn of the eighteenth century,

> being a legal inhabitant of a town involved more than just living within the town limits; a person had to be legally recognized by the selectmen in writing. It was not possible merely to move into a town on one's own volition and thus qualify as an inhabitant. The General Assembly required any new resident in a town who desired to be admitted to furnish written character references from the selectmen of his old town to those of the new town. Only when the selectmen were satisfied with the character of the new resident would he be admitted as an inhabitant [capable thereby of voting at town meetings].[8]

As David Rothman has argued, "The enforcement of settlement laws, which stood midway between poor relief and crime prevention measures, was one basic technique by which colonial communities guarded their good order and tax money."[9]

In the very earliest years of national settlement, citizens created towns in order to improve land, create spaces for commercial development, and control the entrance of unwanted others with access to settlement laws. These formations were generally entrepreneurial. The entrepreneurs, in some cases, were the land companies wishing to plant towns to make enormous profits. In other cases, the entrepreneurs *organized* citizens who were interested in having their own land or church or who were interested in achieving exclusion.

Special districts were not a common phenomenon early in American history, although by the middle of the nineteenth century, developers were using them to create infrastructure and businesses were developing an interest in them.[10] Special districts were created mostly to provide services. Before the Revolution, there were special districts for road repair, bridge building, tobacco house construction and maintenance, and waterways. Some of the earliest districts administered poor relief.[11] In 1768, the Maryland Assembly began creating special districts to fund and administer county almshouses.[12] Before the Revolution, residents of Philadelphia, too, created special districts to govern such things as poor relief and street paving.[13]

The Nineteenth Century

With the opening of the West in the 1800s, the form of the municipality proved to be an exceptional tool for profit. Potential entrepreneurs for the formation of these cities multiplied. While the residents of seventeenth-century Salem Village knew that establishing their own town would enhance property values, nineteenth-century speculators were able to profit handsomely from that knowledge; developers created new cities and imported residents to populate them and make the developers wealthy. Whereas before these were largely land-company-led entrepreneurial efforts, they became developer-controlled efforts. Whereas before the values embedded in the new institutions included exclusion and encouragement of development, the new constellation of values combined those of the developers who desired land improvement and those of the soon-to-be residents who wanted services and prosperity.

The notion that the institutions of the city could provide more favorable taxes and regulations for businesses was also employed more systematically in the nineteenth century. And the forces of class segregation continued to play a role. By the Jacksonian era, however, laws governing the inspection of potential residents had begun to disappear.[14] Note, however, the general absence of most racial motivations. Exclusionary motivations for creating new cities would surface again in the late 1940s.

The Emergence of Services

At the turn of the twentieth century, cities honed their service-delivery functions. Before, they had been able to provide some services, such as fence viewing, but now they could more adequately provide services such as water and electricity.[15] These new services changed the structure and consequences of institutional collective actions dramatically. They increased developers' interest in some forms of local government. They increased citizens' interest in creating new local governments. And they set the stage for heightened concerns about local taxes.

Municipally owned water systems, for example, were developed in the 1830s; St. Louis, Detroit, and Cincinnati had them by 1840.[16] Only eleven cities owned gas works in the late 1800s.[17] As one turn-of-the-century author noted:

> The rapid development of electricity for lighting and other purposes has opened a new field for municipal activity; and the tendency towards the enlargement of municipal functions is strikingly illustrated by the movement for municipal electric lighting.[18]

By 1887 fifty-eight American cities had municipal lighting.[19] Electricity came to Manhattan between 1883 and 1913.[20] The municipally owned street railway, too, became more common in the late 1800s.[21] Sewerage service still had not arrived in large cities such as Mobile and New Orleans by 1898.[22]

Part of the reason for cities' ability to provide these new services was their increased ability to borrow large amounts of money. In the wake of massive state bond defaults in the 1837 financial collapse, states enacted prohibitions on state issuance of railroad bonds. By the late 1900s, railroads had persuaded state legislatures to allow local governments to issue railroad bonds.[23] As Annmarie Hauck Walsh points out, "Enabling legislation for municipal participation in business moved west with the rail-roads."[24] The result was that municipal debt increased from $28 million in 1843 to $1.5 billion in 1900, whereas state debt went from $232 million to $235 million over the same period.[25] Thus, cities acquired an enhanced and more visible ability to fund the services that they now had the technology to provide.[26] As a partial consequence of this coincidence of funding and technology, around the turn of the twentieth century there was a rapid increase in entrepreneur-led service incorporations.

In addition, there was a rapid increase in the formation of special districts at the turn of the century. Like municipalities, special districts could fund and provide the services that citizens demanded more and more insistently. In the late nineteenth century, a number of states established irrigation districts.[27] California authorized the formation of irrigation districts in 1887; these districts bought canals from failing canal companies and were "legal investments for savings banks, trust companies, trust funds, and insurance companies . . . the bonds and their income were exempt from state personal property taxes and from federal income tax."[28] Residents of other states—as different as Mississippi and Massachusetts—also turned to special districts for services.[29] These institutions could embody the (uncompromised) values of developers.

In the wake of a series of municipal defaults on their own oversubscribed-to railroad bonds, state legislatures placed various limitations upon the kinds and levels of debt cities could incur. In 1897, Spokane, Washington, introduced a new form of bond—the revenue bond. These bonds provided a way to fund services even in the face of the new state-imposed debt limits.[30] Instead of being guaranteed by the full faith and credit of the government issuing the bonds, these bonds were "payable solely from the system's revenues, without recourse to the city's taxing powers."[31] This form of financing spread rapidly across the country—to Illinois and Wisconsin in 1899, to Virginia in 1902, to North Carolina in 1903, and to Pennsylvania in 1907.[32] The access to this form of financing made special districts even more appealing to potential entrepreneurs and small groups.

Redefining Cities

In addition to their increasing capacity to provide services in the late nineteenth century, cities gained an important additional measure of autonomy that they did not previously have—autonomy that would

increase entrepreneurial interest in cities. Before this time, state legislatures could alter any aspects of a municipal government; they could
remove officials, alter municipal structure, and award franchises for services.[33] Common wisdom is that residents of cities resented this intru-
sion.[34] An early study of this phenomenon, however, notes that these
interferences were promoted by state legislators from the municipality
and were generally unopposed by the other state legislators—"special
legislation means in fact legislation by the local political clique or
boss."[35] As Henry C. Murphy, a delegate to the New York State Constitutional Convention of 1846, argued, a special act municipal charter

> is a piece of empiricism by the wiseacres of the place where it is to
> be put in force. After being prepared at home, it is sent to the legis-
> lature to be passed. When it reaches that body, no one except the rep-
> resentative from that locality cares what it contains. It is thus left in
> charge of the same interest as that which prepared it.[36]

Murphy challenged the other delegates to provide instances that would
contradict his claim; none did. As a result of this practice, he continued,

> every city may be said to be a law unto itself; and the sovereignty of
> the state, instead of being exercised in its behalf, is absolutely sur-
> rendered to it, to be used at its own discretion.[37]

Borrowing from James Bryce's classic work on American democracy,
The American Commonwealth, Thomas C. Devlin noted in 1896 that

> The city "professionals" will be in attendance at each session of the
> legislature, and when the city charter is acted upon, or special acts
> concerning the city passed, they will be marked by their cunning and
> avarice.[38]

In the late nineteenth century, too, cities turned to special legislation
to avoid the burdens of debt: "when the fire engine [financed by issuing municipal bonds] burned up, or the railroad [financed by municipal
bonds] never got built . . . [l]egislators quickly voted cities out of existence to frustrate repayment or lawsuits."[39] Duluth, Minnesota, was overly
optimistic about the amount of bonded debt that it issued; by the 1870s,
citizens were considering repudiating the debt. Instead, they arranged for
a special act of the legislature to create a new village out of most of the
city. The legislature declared that the village would not be responsible
for the city's debts. Furthermore, the city's creditors could only seek
repayment from the *city's* mayor. The legislature ended the term of the

current mayor and did not set up any mechanism to select a new mayor. Thus, creditors had no legal recourse.[40] Memphis similarly had the Tennessee state legislature reorganize it into a taxing district in 1879.[41]

To be sure, there were interesting abuses of special legislation; nevertheless the source of the abuse seems generally to be the political force in the municipality to be tampered with or a resident of the city. A typical list of abuses is the following:

> The charter of Jersey City was revised ninety-one times by state legislative action between 1835 and 1876. The date of the municipal elections in St. Paul was changed three times in four years by the state. In 1878 Pennsylvania passed a law making legal the stealings of the Philadelphia collector of delinquent taxes. . . . Vanderbilt put through a bill (1872) requiring New York City to pay him $4 million to improve the New York Central tracks on Park Avenue.[42]

Clearly, two of the abuses that Griffith notes here may simply have been routine responses to requests from local officials who could not do these things on their own.

As Jon Teaford has pointed out, special legislation meant that cities had two rulers—the local political officials and the local delegation to the state legislature. Party activity on clearly partisan issues affecting local government was the only force that interfered with this local dominance over special legislation, and even these breakdowns in dominance were exceedingly rare (though more common with respect to New York City than any other city in the country).[43]

In order for a city to serve business interests most effectively, both the local political system and the state legislative representatives had to be controlled by businesses (or any other organizations interested in using the form of the city for their own purposes). With the abolition of special legislation in some states and with the increase in (at least nominal) home rule, cities became a more valuable and more easily controllable form.[44] Home rule gave them more power, and the abolition of special legislation consolidated that power.[45] It created an important space for local autonomy and it increased the incentives to create new cities, incentives that would eventually enable race to matter in the creation of new cities in the United States.

Quite interestingly, southern states tended not to partake of these constitutional changes. As one 1940 author noted, "The Old South did not seem to demand relief from state centralization, partly because the cities relied upon the states to insure their freedom from Negro interference."[46] Immediately after the demise of the Republicans in North Carolina, the state legislature passed a law that

> provided that the legislature should name the justices of the peace, who in turn were to elect the commissioners of their respective counties, thus making the principal county officers appointive. By this means the "black" counties of the east were assured white government. . . . The corresponding device in Louisiana was even simpler. In the hands of the governor . . . was placed "an inordinate appointive power." He appointed the police jury of every parish, which levied local taxes and enacted local laws, as well as all rural school boards, all executive boards and boards of trustees of state institutions, numerous judges, and all registrars, who passed upon the eligibility of voters.[47]

And in Florida, with the rise to power of Redeemer whites who intended to restore white, state-controlled government in southern states after the pull-out of federal troops,

> the successors to Carpetbag rule . . . discovered in the Republican Constitution of 1868 an instrument so well adapted to their purposes that they successfully resisted all attempts to change it for eight years after Redemption. The constitution placed in the hands of the governor the power to appoint (with confirmation by the senate) in each county the tax collector and assessor, treasurer, surveyor, superintendent of schools, county commissioners, sheriff, clerk of court, county judge, and justices of the peace—thus leaving to the uninhibited franchise of free Floridians the choice of constables.[48]

An alternative hypothesis for the lack of such legislation in the South rests on the observation that there were simply fewer and weaker political bosses in the cities there than in the cities of other regions. Monkkonen argues that southern cities remained dominated by commercial leaders or wealthy landowners well after other regions had full-fledged bosses.[49] Grantham points out that due to the mechanisms of disenfranchisement, the southern urban electorate at the turn of the twentieth century was "relatively homogeneous and increasingly middle- and upper-class in makeup."[50] In fact, just after the one period in the nineteenth century when Memphis was faced with enfranchisement of its African-American and lower class residents, the commercial establishment pushed the state legislature to convert Memphis from a city into a nonparticipatory taxing district.[51] (Memphis' African-American population would be enfranchised in the early 1900s through the efforts of Boss Ed Crump.)

The abolition of special legislation also meant the broader establishment of general procedures for incorporation and, in some cases, general procedures for forming various types of special districts.[52] For the states that had this prohibition against special legislation, then, there was now a much simpler process for creating a city (and, in some instances, for creating special districts). The laws were written spelling out the procedure by which citizens could create their own municipality (and, again, in some instances, their own special district). These enabling laws lowered the costs of forming new governments. Moreover, the prohibition against special legislation set the stage for the passage of many special district enabling laws in some states.

The fact of incorporation was crucial for potential entrepreneurs and was a circumstance not generally present before the 1800s. The corporate form was necessary for even mundane functions like uncontested ownership of property. In 1811, for example, the court declared a gift of land to the people of unincorporated Cooperstown, New York, as a site for a courthouse and jail invalid; the court stated that the people of the county did not have the power to own land.[53]

The final important change that occurred during this period was the definition of the city itself. By granting home rule and abolishing special legislation, cities became more stable entities than they had been previously. The definition of the structure was almost entirely in place. At almost the same time, however, considerable debate arose concerning the source of these entities' power. On the one hand, Judge Thomas Cooley (one of the era's leading scholars of constitutional law) argued that cities received power directly from the people and thus they had a kind of limited autonomy:

> the sovereign people had delegated only part of their sovereignty to the states. They preserved the remainder for themselves in written and unwritten constitutional limitations on governmental actions. One important limitation was the people's right to local self-government.[54]

On the other hand, John Dillon (the foremost bond lawyer of his day) argued that cities were creatures of the state—nothing more than administrative divisions. Their authority came solely as a grant from the state.[55] As creatures of the states, these governments had no autonomy. Interestingly, Dillon's argument survived (displacing the very widely read and subscribed-to work of Cooley), while at the same time states granted ever more autonomy to the cities that were their creatures. The results were (1) that states remained able to define and alter local governments in important but general ways but (2) that local government powers were nevertheless quite extensive.[56] Entrepreneurial incentives for creating new cities were now quite high.

Early-Twentieth-Century Districts

Several states tinkered with special districts during the first half of the twentieth century. In 1920, for example, there were seventy-nine levee districts and fifty-eight drainage districts in Texas.[57] Drainage districts were common in other states beginning around 1910.[58] And New York developers used special districts they acquired through special acts of the legislature to "vacate streets" for development.[59]

However, it was in the 1930s that these districts began to be used on a grand scale. First, Franklin Delano Roosevelt pointed out the benefits of the districts as a way to avoid municipal defaults during the Depression; in 1934 he sent a letter to governors urging them to create public corporations that could employ revenue bonds.[60] He urged the creation of water, sewer, and electric light and power districts. He explicitly argued that these governments should be used to circumvent debt limits and referendum requirements for the issuing of bonds.[61] He also dispersed model enabling legislation for housing authorities and soil conservation districts.[62] The U.S. Agriculture Department in the 1930s distributed model soil conservation district enabling legislation and encouraged states to enact this legislation. The Department of Agriculture did this to force co-operation among farmers with the Department's soil conservation efforts; the special districts had coercive powers. Members of Congress from agricultural areas—and the chair of the House Agriculture Committee in particular—provided the impetus behind the Department's support of soil conservation districts.[63] Roosevelt also set up housing legislation such that the receipt of federal funding required a local housing authority.[64] The result was many new special districts. The number of special district formations jumped dramatically in the 1930s.[65] States that prohibited special legislation passed numerous general enabling laws; states that did not prohibit special legislation generally passed only one or two— typically, a general act to create soil conservation districts and a general act to create housing authorities. The costs of forming new districts were thus considerably lower for some would-be solvers of collective action problems.

More Established Entrepreneurs

After World War II, local governments refined their existing purposes and developed a few new ones. Businesses—manufacturing establishments especially—were now even more capable of choosing from among a variety of potential locations for their plants.[66] Transportation links were now available enough to enable businesses to locate manufacturing plants in the largely right-to-work South and corporate headquarters in the communication centers of the North. With that choice, manufacturers could enhance their positions by choosing states with low corporate taxes and by organizing local governments such that they levied few taxes. Moreover, developers broke from other builders in the late 1940s to form their own national organization; in addition, they developed professional journals and their own research organization (the Urban Land Institute).[67] With the sharing of information came the understanding that special districts could effectively provide desired land improvements that would make developments possible and profitable—at no cost to the developer except that of encouraging the creation of the district. The solution to the collective action problem of special district formation shifted definitively to the developers.

Cities and Racial Division

Municipalities also became more effective means of excluding African-Americans from white neighborhoods and white politics in the late 1940s.[68] Before turning to cities for racial exclusion, white citizens used a number of mechanisms to ensure that their neighbors and politics would be exclusively white and sometimes exclusively Protestant.

As discussed above, for example, one of the first actions of southern "Redeemer" governments was to ensure white political control of all local governments, especially those in predominantly African-American counties. The Redeemer governments centralized the selection of local officials to forestall the possibility of African-American political control. In Chapter 2 I noted one nineteenth-century racially motivated attempt to form a city. White Atlanta businessmen wanted to create an African-American city near Atlanta. This effort occurred during the one span of pre-1950 southern history when racially motivated efforts to form southern cities made sense. Once the southern governments were "redeemed," of course, African-Americans were even more completely excluded from southern politics by white primaries, poll taxes, literacy tests, and violence. Racially exclusive southern cities were unnecessary.

Outside of the South, white citizens seemed to desire racial integration or African-American political power no more than did their southern counterparts. To ensure that their neighborhoods were exclusively white, these white citizens organized to spread restrictive deed covenants.

The practice of using race-restrictive covenants generally arrived in a nonsouthern city with African-Americans.[69] Long and Johnson describe these covenants in their 1947 study:

> The race restrictive housing covenant is a mutual agreement entered into by a group of property owners not to sell, rent, lease, or otherwise convey a property to Negroes or other particular minorities. The agreement frequently includes not only the individual property owners, but other cooperating parties as well, such as a real estate board or exchange or a neighborhood improvement association.[70]

Organizing to establish these covenants was done through existing neighborhood improvement associations and with the assistance of businesses—much the same process that later city foundings would employ.[71] The real estate industry provided assistance. The National Association of Real Estate Boards (NAREB) 1943 publication, "Fundamentals of Real Estate Practice," noted:

> The prospective buyer might be a bootlegger who would cause considerable annoyance to his neighbors, a madam who had a number of Call Girls on her string, a gangster who wants a screen for his activities by living in a better neighborhood, *a colored man of means who was giving his children a college education and thought they were entitled to live among whites.* . . . No matter what the motive or character of the would-be purchaser, if the deal would instigate a form of blight, then certainly the well-meaning broker must work against its consummation.[72]

The brokers did. Nevertheless, the Supreme Court declared this mode of excluding African-Americans and other minorities from white neighborhoods and cities unconstitutional in 1948.[73] A new mechanism for racial exclusion outside the South was immediately available: the city and its power to zone.[74] This change meant that legal exclusion would now be limited to groups who were poorer than the group doing the excluding. Restrictive covenants had been used to exclude a variety of groups—Catholics, Jews, African-Americans, and Chinese-Americans, for example. Now the city would turn its exclusionary ability to the poor and to those African-Americans who could be excluded on the basis of poverty.

Cities had been able to zone since 1916, when a combination of New York City's Fifth Avenue landowners and urban reformers imported zoning from Germany and tailored it to suit their purposes. The landowners wanted to prevent garment factories from moving farther up Fifth Avenue by creating a zoning district that excluded them. The reformers wanted to use zoning to exclude skyscrapers and tightly packed buildings. They worried that these two types of buildings would remove sunlight from the city and exacerbate the city's health problems. The rhetoric of the reformers justified the passage of state legislation enabling cities to zone. But the landowners' interests in exclusion and property values soon dominated in zoning practice. Eventually Frederick Law Olmsted would argue that zoning was intended "to give stability to [a district's] . . . property values."[75]

The reformers were able to place zoning within the purview of a city's police power. This was crucial because it meant that zoning was not eminent domain; it was not the taking of private property and thus required no compensation to the property owner.[76]

Almost immediately after its introduction in New York City, zoning spread to the rest of the United States; by 1930 there were 800 zoned municipalities in the country.[77] Part of the cause of this rapid spread was the concern of zoning proponents in New York City that a single city with zoning power would be more judicially vulnerable than would be many cities with zoning power: "Bassett and Lawson Purdy reasoned that since the courts' acceptance of the foundation 'depended to a large extent on the general use and application of that form of regulation, we ought to spread zoning throughout the country.'"[78] In 1924, the Harding administration dispersed general enabling legislation for zoning; within one year of the legislation's release, one-quarter of the states had passed enabling legislation.[79]

Even in early discussions of zoning, proponents recognized it as a plausible substitute for deed covenants.[80] Some early proponents of zoning legislation immediately seized upon the idea as a means to institute "white and Negro residential areas"; this was declared unconstitutional in 1917 as an infringement of the "constitutional right of the white seller to select his buyer."[81]

In 1926 the Supreme Court gave permanence to zoning when it declared zoning to be a reasonable exercise of the city's police power. Foreshadowing one potential future for zoning, one of the first requests for a copy of the Supreme Court's opinion came from the White People's Protective League.[82] By 1920, scholars had become concerned that

> [city] planners and zoning experts often appeal to their clients, that zoning for height and lot area, and sometimes other items, will protect them from "undesirable neighbors." In fact, all the arguments adduced to show that zoning protects property values are meaningless unless they imply this important element in the determination of values. No height restriction, street width or unbuilt lot area will prevent prices from tottering in a good residential neighborhood unless it helps at the same time to keep out Negroes, Japanese, Armenians, or whatever race most jars the natives.[83]

Conclusion

The 320 years between 1630 and 1950 exhibited significant change in the meaning of the boundaries of cities and, to a much lesser extent, of special districts.

Early in this history, new towns could be defensive fortresses. New cities (and, in the early decades, new towns) were also seen as effective providers of lower taxes. In the earlier period, citizens could use the limited autonomy granted to local governments to restrict access to the city to those who would not prove chargeable to the town in order to keep their taxes low and maintain social order. In the later period, zoning could accomplish this. With the outlawing of racially restrictive deed covenants in 1948, cities themselves were the only legal means of ensuring racial homogeneity.

New cities varied in their ability to provide services, largely with changes in the technology of large-scale service provision (but lately, as we will see in Chapter 5, with citizens' desire that these new cities provide only minimal services). Early cities could provide fence viewing; turn-of-the-twentieth-century cities could provide sewerage; and cities in the late 1960s could provide social services. The fact that cities could levy taxes and issue general obligation bonds enabled this service provision. With the development of home rule, the abolition of special legislation in some states, and the passage of general enabling laws for municipal incorporation in the nineteenth century, the city became a more accessible and more valuable instrument to achieve citizens' and entrepreneurs' goals.

Special districts have largely been service providers over the entire course of this history. Sometimes they have been effective providers of access to eminent domain. But, by and large, they have simply funded and provided services. Their ability to do this was much enhanced by the development of the revenue bond in the late 1800s. Citizens turned to these districts more often in states that outlawed special legislation in the late 1800s; passing a single enabling law for a special district meant passing an enabling law for an entire class of districts in those states.[84] Thus, California has an abundance of general enabling laws, whereas Georgia has very few. Citizens formed the districts more insistently after Roosevelt's efforts to point out the ways in which these districts' power to issue revenue bonds could protect local government in the 1930s from default. These districts did not see their heyday in the Progressive Era; they were not, at least not on a grand scale, formed to "remove issues from politics" and to improve the efficiency of local government. Their widespread formation was far more instrumental: They could fund and provide services, provide access to eminent domain, and—sometimes—enforce cooperation and build walls against unfriendly business regulation and taxation. That they also changed the scope of political conflict was a by-product.

4

Elements of Collective Action

> Those who would plan a town must have regard to the spiritual uses
> of what they would cause to be made.
>
> G. D. H. COLE, 1921

The examples presented thus far contain too few cases of failed efforts, and no cases in which citizens did not even try to form governments, for us to know whether the common features in the cases are, in fact, the *reasons* why these new governments formed. The cases do provide important suggestions, however, about what might make citizens, existing organizations, small groups, and entrepreneurs want to form a government and actually succeed in doing so. The cases provide the important details of politics—pictures of the entrepreneurs, organizations, and small groups that are imperfectly captured by the aggregate measures used in the following analyses. As a consequence, they provide the justification for the model specifications I present in this chapter and employ in the next. The quantitative work is necessary, too, because it avoids the pitfalls of selection bias that are inherent in case studies of government formation, and because it can provide insights into the extent to which the findings of these particular cases can be generalized.

Complicating the Argument

Historical factors make cities and special districts more and less capable of different functions at different historical moments. For example, cities have always been useful for altering tax structures. However, these governments became capable of providing most services only at the turn of the twentieth century.

These historical influences did not become static in 1950. We should, therefore, expect some reasons for the formation of new cities and special districts to vary over the course of the three and a half decades of the analyses in Chapter 5.

Three factors—the outlawing of race-restrictive deed covenants in 1948, the expanded scope of post–World War II business location decisions, and the professionalization of real estate developers—differentiated the 1950s from the preceding decades. Two other factors changed over the decades between 1950 and 1987—the fiscal circumstances facing local governments and the characteristics of racial politics. In Chapter 3, I discussed the outlawing of race-restrictive deed covenants. I will address the other factors here.

Developers and Manufacturers in Post–World War II America

In the 1950s developers were just establishing themselves, having split from other builders in the late 1940s to form their own professional organization. They developed methods of professional communication, journals that facilitated the spread of support for special district formation, and a research arm to explore less expensive, less risky means of financing development.[1]

Manufacturing establishments were taking advantage of an even more national economy; business location decisions now encompassed a wider array of options than ever before. Businesses could locate headquarters in New York City to capture the benefits of communication and industrial plants in the rural South to capture the benefits of inexpensive, non-union labor in right-to-work states.[2]

Moreover, in the 1940s and 1950s, businesses had more reasons to start migrating from the central cities to other locations.

> Their production facilities were multistory loft buildings and old plants which the Depression and later World War II (in the case of nondefense plants) had prevented from being reorganized and recapitalized. Their locations were often congested. With the advent of postwar prosperity, with the negative political legacy of the central cities, and with the political and physical *tabula rasa* provided by the suburbs, relocation became the logical choice. Even during World War II, plants funded by the War Production Board were located disproportionately in suburban sites. After 1946, manufacturing employment suburbanized even faster than residential population.[3]

Other newer manufacturing enterprises—defense-related industries and electronics, for example—also began industrial plant establishment during and after the war. Mostly they chose suburbs, and often they chose suburbs in the South and West.[4] Manufacturers, then, were even less trapped in particular locations than they had been before 1950. They could be even pickier. They could more easily locate outside of existing cities—in unincorporated areas in states where corporate taxes were low. The locational advantages of older cities had by and large disappeared.

The Fiscal Circumstances of Local Governments

Two important changes affected cities' financial circumstances. First, there was (1) a dramatic increase in external money going to cities for a wider range of programs in the 1960s, (2) a subsequent refocusing of that funding more exclusively on development, and (3) the eventual slow withdrawal of those sources of external support. Second, there was the beginning of a reason for a tax revolt at the local level. In the end, the tax revolt would prompt two important shifts. Cities would become increasingly less willing to foot the bill for expensive annexations of properties developers were interested in improving. Developers would have greater incentive to turn to special districts. Citizens would also begin to turn to cities almost exclusively for their ability to keep their taxes low.

In the 1950s, the federal government was less involved in local politics than in any later decade. Urban policy focused on developmental policy, mostly alterations of the housing policies enacted in the 1930s and 1940s. The efforts in the 1950s shifted federal housing policy to accommodate the wishes of private developers. The federal government provided money for urban renewal, money that increased over the course of the decade.[5]

In the 1960s, the federal government became more involved in urban problems, initially under the direction of Kennedy and then much more fully under Johnson. The federal government was now interested in an explicitly urban policy. The government's focus expanded from its largely developmental one to cover a much broader array of interests and concerns. During his presidential campaign, John F. Kennedy argued that many local problems were national problems—that "bad housing, poverty, recessions, discrimination, crowded and obsolete schools and hospitals and libraries, inadequate recreation, the breakdown of mass transportation, polluted air and water, juvenile delinquency" were problems that had to be addressed by the federal government.[6] Under the direction of Robert C. Weaver, Kennedy's Housing and Home Finance Agency devised an ambitious plan for urban renewal, public housing, and urban transportation. One part of this, the 1961 Housing Act, passed. This bill funded 100,000 public housing units.[7] In addition, Congress reauthorized urban renewal under Kennedy; the reauthorized program required even less money to be used for projects that were primarily residential. Kennedy also tried unsuccessfully to establish a cabinet-level department for cities.

With the advent of the Johnson presidency, the federal government entered fully into the business of funding and encouraging local governmental redistributive programs. There were plans for poverty programs, Model Cities, expanded mass transit, aid to education, job training, and rent supplements.[8] Johnson was able to establish a cabinet-level post for the cities. Grants-in-aid to local governments increased dramatically.[9] Between 1965 and 1969 federal aid to local governments almost doubled.[10] One result of these programs was to change expectations about exactly what functions local governments were supposed to provide.[11] In addition to being vehicles for development, they seemed now more capable than at almost any other time in the twentieth century—as a consequence of federal efforts—of providing more fully redistributive programs. This shift had the clear potential to increase incentives to create new exclusionary cities, cities that would not have public housing or services for anyone other than the middle or upper middle class.

These changes probably would not have mattered much for the creation of new cities had they not been coupled with an increase in local taxes. Beginning in 1961, states and cities began the largest series of tax increases since the 1930s. With—as some have argued—baby boomers' public schooling bills coming due, state and local governments spent the next fifteen years raising taxes.[12] The incentives to create a new city as a wall against the taxes of another city were increasing.

In the 1970s, the involvement of the federal government shifted away from the redistributive, categorical grants of the 1960s back to more developmental initiatives. Nixon encouraged the trend toward developmental involvement by consolidating numerous categorical grant programs into block grants for local governments. The federal government began limiting its oversight of the way in which these funds were dispersed, thus increasing local discretion concerning the funds' dispersal. The result was that local governments funded fewer and fewer social service and redistributive programs in preference for development.

In particular, Nixon pressed for a reworking of the federal system—for general revenue sharing—which would mean that the federal government would raise money and local governments would decide how to spend that money within broad categorical outlines. This program funded only general-purpose local governments, not the special districts favored by the Johnson-era programs.[13]

Carter attempted to redirect aid to needy cities. He established the Urban Development Action Grant Program (UDAG). And he changed the formula for the Community Development Block Grant Program to shift money to cities that were losing population—northern central cities.[14] But a faltering economy, a tax revolt, and Carter's difficulties in dealing with Congress resulted in smaller increases in programs to benefit local governments during his administration. Aid to local governments still increased, but by smaller amounts than previously, rising by about $30 billion. Social welfare and transportation funding increases constituted about 90% of that $30 billion.[15] With the cuts, though, developers sensed (and experienced) decreased access to municipal funding.[16] Their incentives to turn from cities to special districts for infrastructure were increasing.

Ronald Reagan's 1980 Republican convention acceptance speech forebode bigger changes in relations between the federal government and local governments. He said:

> I believe it is clear our federal government is overgrown and overweight. . . . I will not accept the excuse that the federal government has grown so big and powerful that it is beyond the control of any president, any administration, or Congress. We are going to put an end to the notion that the American taxpayer exists to fund the federal government.
>
> Everything that can be run more effectively by state and local government we shall turn over to state and local government, along with the funding sources to pay for it. We are going to put an end to the money merry-go-round where our money becomes Washington's money, to be spent by the states and cities exactly the way federal bureaucrats tell them to.[17]

The Reagan administration continued to consolidate categorical grants into block grants, but with a very different purpose than that of Nixon.

Nixon had wanted to rationalize government. Reagan wanted to get rid of it. In creating block grants out of categorical ones, the Reagan administration reduced local government funding by 10–35%.[18] Local governments would now be more responsible for raising money to support a whole range of programs.

Cities had been facing tax revolts that cut off funding from below; now they faced more severe constraints from above. Incentives to create cities as hedges against higher taxes had been growing since the early 1960s—well before the famed tax revolts of the 1970s. The federal government simply exacerbated those incentives.

The Changing Relationship Between Race and Local Government

Racial factors changed over these three and a half decades for four reasons: (1) the introduction of the Voting Rights Act, (2) the increasing ability of African-Americans to move to the suburbs in the 1970s, (3) the increasing size of the Latino population in the United States, and (4) the existence of the civil rights movement. I discuss these developments chronologically.

African-Americans continued to move to the North and to the cities during the 1950s. A total of 1.45 million African-Americans moved north in the 1950s.[19] White suburbanization was in full force. Between 1950 and 1970, more than 12 million whites moved out of central cities.[20] Five million mostly southern African-Americans moved to the central cities in the same period.[21]

The civil rights movement began in the early 1950s.[22] Events such as the Montgomery bus boycott in 1955, the *Brown v. Topeka Board of Education* Supreme Court decision in 1954, and the lunch counter sit-ins in Wichita and Oklahoma City in 1958 marked increasing African-American demands for political and economic equality.[23] This movement—and the *Brown* decision in particular—would initially heighten the possibilities for whites to form cities to achieve racial exclusion.

In the 1960s, people moving to the suburbs were still largely white. Moreover, the suburbs were still growing faster than the central cities.[24] However, there was a drop in the migration of African-Americans from the South to the North.[25]

The civil rights movement continued to develop in the 1960s. There were lunch counter sit-ins at the beginning of the decade, riots throughout the decade that increased in frequency toward the late 1960s, the Missis-sippi Freedom Summer, the Selma campaign, and the dramatic extension of African-American voter registration.[26] Racially exclusionary cities would stay on some whites' agendas even as African-Americans chal-lenged racially exclusionary politics more generally.

African-Americans won a significant victory when Congress enacted the Voting Rights Act in 1965 to remove impediments to African-Ameri-can registration and voting. This law contained a provision—Section 5—that required Justice Department monitoring of changes in institu-tions or laws affecting elections in all counties in the United States with low voter registration and with a test or other restriction on voter regis-tration. New criteria for monitoring would go into effect in 1970 and 1975.[27] With the introduction of the Voting Rights Act, mechanisms to achieve racial exclusion were abolished in states ranging from Missis-sippi to Alaska. Prior to its enactment, state-level controls on political participation had made local politics an all-white, relatively affluent affair in some states. After its enactment, state-enforced racial exclusion from local politics was outlawed, thus altering legal participation in local gov-ernments and transferring to covered jurisdictions a local institutional function that had by and large been absent from *and* redundant in states where African-Americans were already excluded from political partici-pation.

The Voting Rights Act also made forming a new government—a municipality or a special district—more difficult. Formation now required preclearance by the Justice Department. This meant that any change that might affect elections had to be submitted for prior approval to the Justice Department, along with documentation concerning the potential effects of the change upon African-American political power. The law was enacted in 1965. However, full procedures for implementing Section 5 were not developed for several years.[28]

The Voting Rights Act had two potential influences upon government formation. It increased incentives to form racially exclusive cities in covered jurisdictions. It also made it more difficult to form both cities and special districts by increasing the monitoring of both motivations for and effects of the creation of new governments.

In the 1970s there was still a movement to the suburbs; suburbs grew by 20 million people, but cities grew by only 3 million during the decade.[29] Suburbanization was beginning to change a little. African-Americans joined the movement to the suburbs.[30] Between 1970 and

1980, for example, the African-American population of suburban counties around Washington, D.C., increased dramatically; some counties experienced as much as a 170% increase in their African-American population.[31] Whereas in 1970 the African-American suburban population in the Washington, D.C., area was 166,033, by 1980 it had increased to 390,077. At the same time, the African-American population of the District of Columbia itself had decreased by 88,806.[32] In part, this movement was facilitated by the passage of the Fair Housing Act of 1968, which prohibited discrimination in the sale or rental of housing.[33] More generally, there seem to have been two patterns of African-American suburbanization. Outside the South, as Logan and Schneider point out, African-Americans who suburbanized generally moved to suburbs where African-Americans already lived. In the South, when African-Americans suburbanized, they did not necessarily move only to suburbs with large African-American populations.[34] Zoning was losing its power as an exclusionary tool as more African-Americans moved into the middle-class and relocated to suburbs.[35] One court decision, in particular, began to diminish the power of exclusionary zoning, at least in New Jersey: the Mount Laurel II decision requiring New Jersey localities to zone for low- and moderate-income housing.[36] This power of zoning had previously been the reason why the form of the city could be used to ensure racial exclusion. Racial exclusion should have diminished or disappeared as a reason to form cities in the 1970s and 1980s.

However, with the increasing Latino population in the United States—a population that did not have nearly as large a middle class as did African-Americans in the 1980s—we might expect the emergence of an ethnically exclusionary function for the city in the 1980s, this time along Latino/Anglo lines.[37]

Services

Service reasons should remain consistently important throughout. However, with the increasing fiscal strain on cities, we might expect two consequences. First, developers—particularly in areas where tax bases are limited—should turn even more insistently to special districts for infrastructure funding. Second, citizens should form fewer and fewer cities out of a desire to acquire services, as they have to pay more and more for those service-providing cities and as they engage in tax revolts at the local level.

Therefore, although the broad picture of local government formation should remain the same throughout the three and a half decades, the details of the particular uses of these institutional forms should shift with changing federal and state policies, with changing African-American affluence and political power, and perhaps with Latino immigration. The main source of continuity throughout should be entrepreneurial and group desires to use the institutional forms of cities and special districts to enhance profits and lower costs. Without these entrepreneurs and groups, some forces would lose their importance in the formation of local governments and other forces' importance would be diminished.

Measurement

The analyses in the next chapter assess this argument through quantitative analyses of government formations (and the lack thereof) in 200 U.S. counties. Because of the changing politics just discussed, I divide the analyses into decades—for example, an analysis of special district formation in the 1950s, an analysis of municipal formation in the 1950s, an analysis of special district formation in the 1960s, and so on.[38]

Here I will simply present the measures I use to operationalize the argument. I present the full justification of these measures in Appendix B. I urge readers to read this appendix; it provides them with the ability to evaluate more fully and more independently the results I present in Chapter 5. Keep in mind that the measures are aggregate, county-level indicators of the processes occurring within the counties. Their justification rests largely with the work presented in Chapters 2 and 3.

Operationalizing the various pieces of this argument is, by and large, straightforward. Nevertheless, because the analyses address two different types of institutions of local government and cover three and a half decades of American history, there are a few complications. Four of the sixteen indicators noted in Tables 4.1 and 4.2 and discussed more fully in Appendix B have slightly different interpretations for the two types of governments. These differences result solely from the differences between special districts and municipalities. Tables 4.1 and 4.2 present the variables I used to operationalize the argument.

The dependent variables are straightforward. Throughout, they are the number of new governments formed in a particular decade, as reported in the 1987 Census of Governments, Government Organi-

Table 4.1. Variables in the Municipal Analyses

Services	Percentage population change in the previous decade
	Log of the population at the beginning of the decade
	Median family income interacted with corporate tax rate (reversed)
Taxes	Annexation allowed, unilateral (dummy variable)
	Annexation allowed, with at least one citizen defense against annexation (dummy variable)
Race	Number of nonwhite/African-American/Latino residents
	Number of nonwhite/African-American/Latino residents interacted with corporate tax rate (reversed)
Supply	Whether a special act is required to form a municipality (dummy variable)
	Number of general enabling laws for special districts
	Voting Rights Act preclearance coverage (dummy variable)
Entrepreneurs	Whether there is a manufacturer in the county (dummy variable)
	Corporate income tax rate (reversed) interacted with the log of the number of manufacturers
	Tax levy limit (dummy variable)

Note: In the above list, where I noted that a scale is reversed, this simply means that instead of the highest corporate tax rate, for example, being 11 and the lowest being 0, the scale is reversed such that the lowest is given a value of 12 and the highest is given a value of 1. This is done to simplify the presentation in Chapter 5; with the reversal, as the numbers become larger, the incentives for businesses to form governments increase.

Table 4.2. Variables in the Special District Analyses

Services	Percentage population change in the previous decade
	Log of the population at the beginning of the decade
	Tax levy limit (dummy variable)
Race	Number of nonwhite/African-American/Latino residents
	Number of nonwhite/African-American/Latino residents interacted with entrepreneurial conditions (log of the number of real estate and financial concerns in the 1950s; number of developers in later decades)
Supply	Whether a special act is required to form a municipality (dummy variable)
	Number of general enabling laws for special districts
	Voting Rights Act preclearance coverage (dummy variable)
Entrepreneurs and small groups	Number of Developers
	Median family income interacted with entrepreneurial conditions
	Annexation allowed, unilateral (dummy variable)
	Annexation allowed, with at least one citizen defense (dummy variable)

zation Data File. The 1987 census—unlike previous censuses—asked governments when they formed. I used the formation dates to calculate the number of special districts and municipalities that formed in a decade in a county in the sample.[39] Figures 4.1 through 4.8 map the dependent variable for all counties in the United States for each of the decades of the analyses.

Fig. 4.1. New cities, 1952–62 (randomly distributed within states).

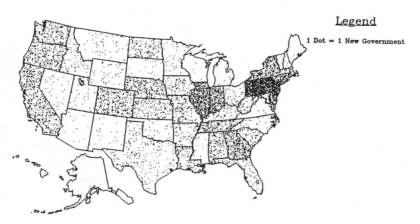

Fig. 4.2. New special districts, 1952–62 (randomly distributed within states).

Fig. 4.3. New cities, 1962–72 (randomly distributed within states).

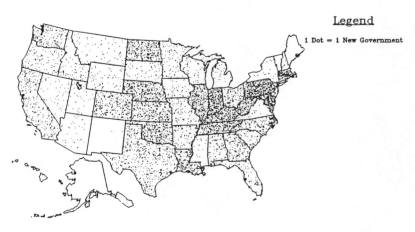

Fig. 4.4. New special districts, 1962–72 (randomly distributed within states).

Fig. 4.5.　New cities, 1972–82 (randomly distributed within states).

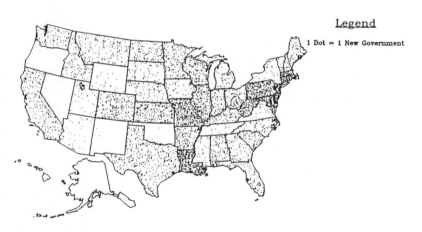

Fig. 4.6.　New special districts, 1972–82 (randomly distributed within states).

Fig. 4.7. New cities, 1982–87 (randomly distributed within states).

Fig. 4.8. New special districts, 1982–87 (randomly distributed within states).

The Sample and the Model

The 200 counties in the sample are a simple random sample of the counties in the United States.[40] I employ a sample of 200 because it allows the detection of relatively small effects with satisfactorily small standard errors. Appendix D contains a list of the counties in the sample. I used the census list of counties from the 1972 *County and City Data Book* as the universe from which to draw the sample. Consequently, one county—Wade Hampton, Alaska—does not exist until the later decades of the study. It enters the analyses in the 1970s. Figure 4.9 maps these counties.

I discuss the methodology I employ in more detail in Appendix B.

Conclusion

The formation of cities and special districts from 1950 through 1987 is a continuation of the earlier processes in the development of local institutions in America.

As with earlier formations, the usefulness of cities and special districts is historically grounded. Reasons for formation thus vary over time.

Fig. 4.9. Actual locations of the counties in the sample.

Several factors cause this variation: the Voting Rights Act; the shift in federal funding to local government beginning in the 1970s; the increasing cost of local government beginning in the 1960s; the growing affluence, suburbanization, and empowerment of African-Americans; and the immigration of Latinos. Some of the sources of change are political—acts of legislatures—and some are demographic.

These historical factors make cities useful for service provision in the 1950s and 1960s, for racial division in the 1950s and 1960s, and for lowering taxes in the 1960s, 1970s, and 1980s. Cities are useful for entrepreneurs—in particular, manufacturing firms—throughout this period because of their ability to provide lower taxes.

Special districts are useful for services throughout. They are useful for developers throughout because of their ability to fund infrastructure, a function that is enhanced with the increasingly tightened local fiscal picture, a picture that restricts the alternative sources of funding for infrastructure.

5

Creating Local Politics

Americans institutionalized racial exclusion, low taxes, and new levels of services in their local governments from the 1950s through the 1980s. This was in many ways a continuation of the politics of government creation from earlier eras. These new governments started the period examined here as ways to get new services and to enforce racial exclusion. They ended as walls against higher taxes and as ways for developers to shift the start-up costs of development. Throughout, the most systematic forces in the creation of these institutions were businesses and developers. Perhaps not surprisingly, these are the same forces that scholars of urban politics find dominate local politics.

Services and Taxes

> The taxpayer is apt, if actuated by selfish motives, to oppose those forms of municipal activity which will involve a considerable expense of money, and to favor such plans as will reduce the tax rate.
> —MILO ROY MALTBIE, 1898[1]

The most obvious and seemingly mundane reason that citizens create new cities and special districts is to gain access to new services—water services, road paving, sewerage systems. These reasons became important at the turn of the twentieth century, when local governments gained access to the technology necessary to provide services such as water and sewerage and special districts gained access to revenue bonds. Service provision continued to be an important reason for forming local governments in the second half of the twentieth century.

Service desires, however, were overshadowed in many instances by citizens' desire to keep their tax burdens low. Initiatives such as California's Proposition 13 and Massachusetts' Proposition 2½ provide obvious examples of citizens' wish for lower taxes. Both citizens and businesses, however, were interested in achieving lower taxes than their neighbors well before these tax revolt initiatives occurred. They used the form of the city to keep themselves from being annexed to older cities that had populations with higher service needs, smaller tax bases, and thus higher taxes. These citizens and businesses were able to define unwanted others out of their politics, creating—in fact—political boundaries that signified class and racial divisions.

Interpretation and Presentation

The results presented here are the results of the estimation of the Poisson regression equations described in Appendix B. The equations are Poisson regressions of the number of either special districts or municipalities formed in a county in a particular decade upon variables indicating desire for services, desire for lower taxes, desire for racial exclusion, conditions amenable to the emergence of political entrepreneurs and small groups, and legal structures of supply. I present these coefficient estimates and their robust standard errors in Appendix C. The coefficient estimates are remarkable in that none of them change in either magnitude or sign over the course of the three and a half decades of analyses.

To make the presentation more accessible, I present the results of these equations in terms of the effects that the explanatory variables have upon the number of new special districts and cities formed in a county in a given decade. A Poisson specification means that the effects of one variable depend upon the values of the other variables in the equation. Consequently, I hold the other variables constant at their means (except when the combination that would result would not be possible) when I evaluate the influence of a particular variable. I calculate the effects of a change from about one standard deviation below the mean of the variable in question to about one standard deviation above the mean. These variables are probably not Normally distributed, so this range is not a constant 68% of the distribution. I use these ranges to provide a sense of the effects of reasonable changes in explanatory variables upon the number of special districts or municipalities created in a county in a given decade. Moreover, since the models are Poisson regressions, not linear-Normal regressions, the actual coefficient estimates cannot be interpreted in the same ways as linear-Normal regression coefficients, as I discuss in the Appendix B. Because the models are interactive, I will describe the results with an eye toward both sorting out the effects of a particular variable and documenting the conditions that allow those effects to materialize.

I am including all of the information necessary for the reader to make her own independent evaluation of these results in Appendix C at the end of the book.

Services

The results reported in Table 5.1 suggest the extent to which citizens formed new cities in order to acquire new services. The numbers in boldface are the numbers of new governments that result from reasonable changes in the specified explanatory variable when I hold all other variables constant at their means. The asterisks indicate the strength of the relationship between the particular independent variable and the num-

Table 5.1. Special Districts and Services

	Effect (Mean of X) [Range Over Which Evaluated] $*p < .10$ $**p < .05$ $***p < .001$			
Variable	1950s	1960s	1970s	1980s
Population change in previous decade	**0.17** (6.7) [−20,34]			
Log of the population at the beginning of the decade	**0.52***** (3) [2,4]	**0.95***** (3) [1,4]	**0.49***** (3) [1.5,4.5]	
Whether a tax levy limit is in effect	**0.68***** (0.02) [0,1]		**0.90** (0.02) [0,1]	

ber of new governments. The number in parentheses just below the effect is the mean value of the explanatory variable. And the number in brackets below the mean is the change in the explanatory variable that yielded the particular change in the number of new governments. So the first cell in Table 5.1 says that the effect of an increase in population is 0.17 new special districts. The mean population growth is 6.7%. And the effect is a result of comparing counties with a population growth of 34% with counties with a population loss of 20% (about one standard deviation above and below the mean). Some cells are empty because the particular explanatory variable was not systematically related to the number of special districts formed in the decade. I explain all of the operationalizations in Appendix B.

The results suggest that citizens succeeded in forming new special districts from the 1950s through the 1970s, in part, because they simply wanted the new services that these governments could provide. By the 1980s—with the increasing expensiveness of local government—citizens were no longer forming special districts to acquire new services.

I measured citizens' desire for services here by population change in the previous decade, by the log of the population at the beginning of the decade, and by the presence of tax levy limits. If, in fact, citizens were forming new districts to provide themselves with more services, these coefficients would be positive. They are. Citizens in counties with larger population increases in the 1940s formed about one-sixth of a special district more than did citizens in counties that did not experience this growth. The mean number of districts formed in a county in the 1950s was 0.88, so this effect is substantively interesting but not huge. Citizens in counties with larger populations formed one-half of a special district more in the 1950s than did citizens in counties with smaller populations. Citizens in counties faced with a tax levy limit formed two-thirds of a special district more than did citizens in other counties. The results *suggest* that citizens formed special districts in the 1950s in part to provide services. These results *suggest* that population pressures led citizens to press for more special districts, as did limits on the funding abilities of existing local governments. Note that citizens formed more districts in areas with large populations than they did in areas with population growth.

In the 1960s and 1970s, citizens continued to form special districts simply to provide services. In the 1960s, larger populations meant twice as many formations as they meant in the 1950s. The average number of new special districts in the 1960s was 1.17, so the effect of population is substantial. And in the 1970s, large populations remained important. Tax levy limits returned to constrain the ability of existing local governments to provide services, perhaps pushing citizens to form special districts, though this effect is not very systematic.

Table 5.2 presents the effects of pressures for new services upon the formation of cities. In the 1950s, citizens formed more cities in counties (1) with significant population growth in the 1940s, (2) where there was a large population in the 1950s, and (3) where there were entrepreneurial incentives combined with high median incomes (though this last effect is not very systematic). As soon as municipalities embarked upon their tax increases of the 1960s, citizens lost interest in new cities' ability to provide services. Only the presence of large populations mattered. And in the 1970s and 1980s, as taxes continued to rise, service desires—at least as measured by these aggregate variables—were unimportant.

In the 1950s, the effect of an increase in population was 0.02 new municipalities; the effect of a large population was 0.03 municipal incor-

Table 5.2. Municipalities and Services

	Effect (Mean of X) [Range Over Which Evaluated] $*p < .10$ $**p < .05$ $***p < .001$			
Variable	1950s	1960s	1970s	1980s
Population change in previous decade	**0.02**** (6.7) [−20,34]			
Log of the population at the beginning of the decade	**0.03*** (3) [2,4]	**0.15***** (3) [1,4]		
Corporate tax rate interacted with median family income Higher taxes Lower taxes	**0.004** **0.02** ($14,037) [median income: $1,495,$3,093]			

porations; and the effect of the presence of high-income populations was (even in combination with low corporate taxes) only 0.02 municipal incorporations. Clearly, none of these effects is particularly large, especially given that the mean number of cities formed in a county was 0.24 in the 1950s. Citizens' desire for new services—as indicated by the effects of population pressures and high incomes—did not contribute heavily to the formation of municipalities in the 1950s. In the 1960s, the effect of a large population was 0.15 new cities. That the other two service variables disappeared from the equation suggests that the last few service formations were suburbs.

Taxes

These aggregate results suggest that citizens' desire for lower taxes began to influence the formation of cities in the 1960s—as local government became more expensive. By the 1980s, walling out higher taxes appears to have been virtually the only reason citizens created new cities. These tax worries quite logically occurred as citizens stopped forming cities to provide new services. Citizens instead formed special districts to acquire new services. By the 1980s, however, worry about taxes overwhelmed both municipal and special district formation.

Citizens' tax worries had their largest effect in the 1960s, when local governments engaged in their biggest tax increases since the 1930s (Table 5.3). Where annexation was legal, and citizens thus had reason to worry about being annexed to existing cities with higher taxes, citizens formed over one-tenth of a new city more than did citizens in counties where annexation was illegal. In the 1970s, these effects were smaller but still substantial. And in the 1980s, the effect was tiny but was the largest of the small influences in the 1980s.

The results here suggest that over these three and a half decades, new cities changed from being providers of services to being providers of lower taxes. The meaning of new city limits changed. Once new cities became potential providers of lower taxes, they became enforcers of class divisions with their power to zone.

Special district formation also changed. Citizens used special districts to provide the services they were unable to acquire from or unwilling to finance through new or existing municipalities. By the 1980s, citizens no longer formed even special districts to acquire new services. Only developers formed them.

Table 5.3. Municipalities and Taxes

Effect
(Mean of *X*)
[Range Over Which Evaluated]
*p < .10 **p < .05 ***p < .001

Variable	1950s	1960s	1970s	1980s
Annexation allowed, unilateral		0.14***	0.05***	
		(0.12)	(0.12)	
		[0,1]	[0,1]	
Annexation allowed, citizens of		0.14***	0.09***	0.01***
area to be annexed have at least		(0.84)	(0.80)	(0.80)
one channel of defense		[0,1]	[0,1]	[0,1]

Race

Along with providing effective mechanisms for class segregation, new cities have provided effective barriers to racial integration. Evidence suggests, in fact, that the boundaries of cities are now more frequently racial boundaries than are neighborhood borders.[2] Cities provide racial boundaries because of their power to zone and because the correlation between race and income enables this zoning power to affect racial composition. In addition, where the presence of an African-American middle class has enabled African-American suburbanization, this movement has largely been to suburbs that already contained African-Americans, thus reinforcing the patterns of racial segregation institutionalized through city boundaries.[3]

Special Districts

Table 5.4 reports the effects of racial composition upon the formation of special districts over the thirty-seven-year period. Race mattered only in the 1950s.

The effects of racial composition in the 1950s depended entirely upon the presence of developers. Where there were few developers, the presence of relatively large African-American populations meant that citizens formed three-quarters of a special district fewer than they did elsewhere. The presence of developers, however, dampened this negative effect. Where there were relatively many African-Americans and where there were also many potential entrepreneurs, only one-half of a special district fewer formed than formed elsewhere. This result represents one of the few times when developers' efforts were truly entrepreneurial—when the values of both the developers and a group of residents were embedded in a new local government.

This result suggests that the combination of entrepreneurs and collective pressures—in this case, racial ones—affected local institutional structures. Alone, the indicator of the collective pressure dampened the formation of new special districts. The entrepreneur seemed to have been able to move the citizens closer to creating new governments.

There are two potential interpretations of this effect. One is that African-Americans wanted services that developers could provide in the pro-development atmosphere of urban renewal politics in the 1950s. The other is that white citizens interested in racial exclusion wished to create less participatory institutions that could diminish African-American

Table 5.4.   Special Districts and Race

	Effect (Mean of X) [Range Over Which Evaluated]			
Variable	1950s	1960s	1970s	1980s
Number of nonwhite residents interacted with the log of the number of financial and real estate concerns				
Few developers	−0.74**			
More developers	−0.57**			
	(23.6) [number of nonwhite residents: 0,28]			
Number of Latino residents				0.08*** (4.83) [0,30]

influence in local politics. The former explanation is more plausible. I will provide additional evidence for this interpretation below.

By the 1960s, however, this effect was gone. Citizens in counties with large African-American populations behaved no differently than did their counterparts. In the 1980s, a variation of this composition effect may have returned, although the evidence is very slight.

In the 1980s, the only indication of continuing citizen interest in forming special districts was that the presence of Latinos led to a small increase in the number of special districts formed. Citizens in counties with 30,000 Latino residents formed 0.08 more special districts than did citizens of counties with no Latino residents.

Perhaps this small effect of the ethnic composition of the population means that these citizens were effectively creating governments to provide services they desired. However, the effect is small and is only suggestive.

Municipalities

The relationship of racial motivations to the formation of cities is more striking. In part, this is simply because cities are more capable of ensuring racially exclusionary politics than are special districts. Cities zone. Citizens, however, were able to take advantage of the racially exclusionary capabilities of new cities only when manufacturers enabled them to do so. I report the results in Table 5.5.

Race had the largest effect upon the formation of municipalities in the 1950s; this effect depended entirely upon the presence of conditions amenable to the emergence of political entrepreneurs. These entrepreneurs were manufacturers who wanted lower taxes and who were willing to sustain a movement for the formation of a new municipality in order to achieve that goal. They enabled race to matter in the formation of cities in the 1950s. Where corporate taxes were relatively high, citizens in counties with 28,000 African-Americans formed one-tenth of a city fewer than did their counterparts in counties with no African-American residents. When corporate taxes were relatively low—and thus entrepreneurial incentives relatively strong—this same comparison led to the formation of *one-quarter* of a new municipality. The effect of this interaction is, in fact, larger than the average number of new cities in counties in the 1950s.

Table 5.5.   Municipalities and Race

Effect
(Mean of X)
[Range Over Which Evaluated]

Variable	1950s	1960s	1970s	1980s
Number of nonwhite residents interacted with corporate tax rate				
Higher taxes	−0.08***	−0.08***		
Lower taxes	0.29***	0.11***		
	(29)	(42.5)		
	[number of nonwhite residents: 0,28]	[number of nonwhite residents: 0,36.5]		
Number of Latino residents				0.004***
				(4.83)
				[0,30]
Number of Latino residents interacted with corporate tax rate				
Higher taxes				0.0007***
Lower taxes				−0.001***
				(41)
				[Number of Latinos: 0,30]

To anticipate the results below concerning the presence of manufac-turers, this combination of low taxes and relatively large African-Ameri-can populations was not effective in creating a municipality where there were no manufacturing firms to take advantage of these conditions. Without manufacturing firms, these conditions led citizens to create 0.00004 (!) more cities. With manufacturing firms to serve as entrepre-neurs, these conditions resulted in the creation of *0.35* more cities.

As with the formation of special districts, there are several potential reasons for this effect. The result could indicate that African-Americans and manufacturers together created cities. Or it could indicate that white citizens interested in racial exclusion combined with manufacturers to create cities that would have the power to zone out those with potentially higher social service needs. In light of the evidence in Chapters 2 and 3, the latter is the more plausible explanation. I will discuss this here and provide more evidence below.

These results suggest that racial concerns may have encouraged citizens to want new cities, but only in the presence of entrepreneurs were citizens with these concerns able to succeed in forming new cities in the 1950s. Moreover, the places with large African-American populations but without entrepreneurs were largely counties that already had state laws to exclude African-Americans from politics. These were counties in states that were covered by Section 5 of the Voting Rights Act beginning in the mid-1960s. This might explain the negative effect of racial composition alone upon the formation of new cities in the 1950s; forming a city for racial reasons would have been redundant. Again, due to the nature of the measures I use here, this result, while striking, is only suggestive. I present more evidence below.

Concern for racial issues—as indicated by racial composition—mattered in roughly the same way in the 1960s as it mattered in the 1950s. Again, the effect of racial composition can only be assessed in combination with the extent to which there were favorable conditions for the emergence of entrepreneurs. Where corporate taxes were high—where there were *unfavorable* conditions for entrepreneurs (as explained in Appendix B)—larger African-American populations meant fewer city formations. Where corporate taxes were low, larger African-American populations led citizens and entrepreneurs to form 0.11 more cities than elsewhere.

The effect of the combination of low corporate taxes and relatively large African-American populations was influenced by the possibility of annexation in the state. Where annexation was possible—where the idea of forming a city could be sparked in part by a neighbor's efforts to annex—the combination of lower corporate taxes and relatively large African-American populations led to 0.16 new cities. Where annexation was illegal—where the idea of forming a city had to be generated, in a sense, independently—this combination led to the formation of a minuscule 0.000006 new cities.

The effect of the combination of race and entrepreneurial conditions, then, is consistent with the argument that entrepreneurs combined with individuals interested in racial exclusion, in some instances, to create cities. They did this almost exclusively in places where annexation could spur them to action—where annexation was legal. I will provide more evidence concerning this interpretation below.

As with the formation of special districts, the presence of Latinos had a positive effect upon the formation of municipalities in the 1980s. However, the effect here is so small as to be substantively irrelevant. Entrepreneurs seemed to dampen this effect slightly—but, again, the effect of the combination of Latino population and an entrepreneur is tiny.

Other Supporting Evidence

There is one useful source of additional evidence concerning the interpretation of these racial composition effects: analyses of the actual and predicted government formations in counties that had entrepreneurs and relatively large African-American populations in the 1950s and 1960s.

Municipalities. In the above analyses, the combination of entrepreneurs and large African-American populations appeared to be potentially potent in the politics of municipal formation in the 1950s and 1960s. I have suggested that city formations resulting from this combination were in part prompted by white citizens interested in forming a new city that could provide racially exclusionary zoning. With their own city, these citizens would be better able to ensure that African-Americans—at least those without a good deal of money—would not move to their neighborhood in the near future. These citizens generally could not create a city on their own. They needed the support of an entrepreneur that would provide the financing and the organization (and a tax base) to sustain their movement to create a city. I have argued that there were many potential sources of these resources for political action but that one systematic source in the post–World War II era was manufacturers. The evidence I have provided is simply that the presence of a large African-American population and low corporate taxes had a large effect upon city creation in the 1950s and 1960s.

The evidence provided thus far regarding the role of race in these formations has been only suggestive. One could develop explanations other than the ones I have presented to explain these results. This section provides additional evidence that lends more credence to the argument presented above. I examine these particular formations in several ways to develop a clearer understanding of the influence of race upon city creations in the 1950s and 1960s. First, I examine the locations of the city incorporations in which the model suggests that racial exclusion played a role. Then I examine the racial composition of these new cities. Finally, I examine the merits of the most plausible competing explanation: that the effects of racial composition are not due to race but rather to pocketbook concerns about the presence of poor populations, without regard to race. In the first two analyses, I focus upon cities where the models predicted formations and these formations occurred. I focus only upon places where the models suggest that racial exclusionary motivations were part of the drive to incorporate.

Where Are These New Cities? If the above reasoning is correct, counties with the combination of relatively large African-American populations and low corporate taxes (1) with actual city formations (2) where the models predicted formations *should not be counties where Section 5 of the Voting Rights Act went into effect in the mid-1960s.* White citizens desiring racial exclusion in those counties covered by Section 5 of the Voting Rights Act in the 1960s had state-level insurance before 1965 that their politics (and neighborhoods) could continue on their racially exclusive track. They did not need to form cities to accomplish this. These counties were the counties where African-American disenfranchisement was widespread and legally supported. Forming a city to ensure a racially exclusive neighborhood would have been redundant. If the argument about the role of racial motivations is correct, these formations, then, should not be in counties where African-Americans could have little political impact.

Table 5.6 presents the results of this examination. *None* of the counties were covered jurisdictions under the Voting Rights Act in the mid-1960s. This provides more suggestive evidence concerning the interpretation of the race variables in the analyses of municipal formations in the 1950s and 1960s. The counties where race mattered were those with the potential for racially inclusive politics. Of course, there remain two plausible reasons for this result: Where African-Americans had the possibility of a political voice, they formed their own cities to exercise that voice; or where African-Americans had the possibility of a political voice, white Americans formed cities to exclude them. The next analysis suggests the latter to be the more plausible interpretation.

Who Lives in These New Cities? There is a second way that we can

Table 5.6.   Counties in Which the Models Suggest
Racially Motivated Formations

Counties with African-American populations larger than the
mean, with entrepreneurial conditions, with local government
formations, and with predicted formations of 0.50 or greater

Municipalities, 1950s

Broward, FL	7 formations	2.39 predicted
Harrison, TX	1 formation	0.60 predicted

Municipalities, 1960s

Broward, FL	8 formations	1.65 predicted
Macomb, MI	1 formation	0.73 predicted
Muskegon, MI	2 formations	0.67 predicted
El Paso, TX	1 formation	0.96 predicted
Harrison, TX	2 formations	0.56 predicted

look at these new cities in order to understand the influence of race. If
the city creations were efforts by African-Americans to gain control of
their politics, the new cities' populations should contain large numbers
of African-Americans. If these city creations were, in part, racially exclusionary efforts to keep politics and neighborhoods white, their populations should be almost exclusively white. If this latter scenario is the case,
the result is suggestive, *given that the counties in which these new cities
were formed had relatively large African-American populations.* Tables
5.7.1 and 5.7.2 report the 1970 racial composition of the cities where the
earlier analyses led us to suspect racially exclusionary motivations. The
counties here are the same as those examined in Table 5.6. The table is
in two parts, one for the 1950s and one for the 1960s. The table presents
the racial composition of the new cities and of the counties in which they
were formed.

There are several important numbers to note in the two parts of Table
5.7. First, compare the populations of the new cities with the number of
African-Americans in these cities. Then look at the percentage of
African-Americans in the new cities. Finally, compare the percentage
of African-Americans in the counties with the percentage of African-
Americans in the new cities formed within these counties.

The results of this series of comparisons are striking. In all cases, the
African-American population of these newly created cities is minuscule

Table 5.7.1.   Racial Composition of These New Cities

1950s	Date Formed	1970 Population	1970 African-American Population	
New Haven, CT		744,948	56,954	7..60%
Milford	1959	50,858	509	1.00
Broward, FL		620,069	77,360	12.50%
Miramar	1955	23,973	14	0.05
Pembroke Park	1957	2,949	3	0.10
Cooper	1959	2,535	1	0.03
Lauderhill	1959	8,465	1	0.01
Lighthouse Point	1956	9,071	1	0.01
Margate	1955	8,829	9	0.10
Plantation	1953	23,523	129	0.55
Harrison, TX		44,841	16,490	36.77%
Waskom	1950	1,460	82	5.62%

to nonexistent (even twenty years after the cities were formed, as with the formations in the early 1950s). In most cases, African-Americans compose far less than 1% of the population of these new cities. Moreover, in all cases, the new cities contain significantly smaller percentages of African-Americans than do the counties in which they were formed.[4]

Again, this evidence is only suggestive. Nevertheless, these results lend more credence to the argument that these cities were formed in part because white citizens wanted to institute racially exclusive politics with the zoning power that these new cities would have.

Is It Really Race, or Is It Simply the Presence of Large, Relatively Poor Populations with High Service Needs? A plausible argument is that the effects I document here are not really *racial* effects, but rather a different manifestation of an economic argument. The plausible alternative would state that these large African-American populations are probably not well off economically and that they might want new or different services from local government. When people form homogeneous white suburbs, the argument would continue, they are simply protecting their

Table 5.7.2.   Racial Composition of These New Cities

1960s	Date Formed	1970 Population	1970 African-American Population	
Broward, FL		620,069	77,360	12.50%
Davie	1961	2,856	9	0.32
Coral Springs	1963	1,489	0	0.00
Lauderdale Lakes	1961	10,577	4	0.03
North Lauderdale	1963	1,212	0	0.00
Parkland	1963	NA	NA	
Sunrise	1961	7,403	1	0.01
Tamarac	1963	5,078	0	0.00
Coconut Creek	1967	1,359	9	0.66
Macomb, MI		625,309	7,570	1.21%
Sterling Heights	1968	61,530	38	0.06
Muskegon, MI		157,426	16,730	10.63%
Norton Shores	1968	22,271	168	0.75
Lakewood Club	1967	590	NA	
El Paso, TX		359,291	10,010	2.79%
Vinton	1961	NA	NA	
Harrison, TX		44,841	16,490	36.77%
Scottsville	1962	NA	NA	
Uncertain	1965	NA	NA	

Source: U.S. Department of Commerce. 1970. *1970 Census of Population: Characteristics of the Population*, v. 1. Washington, DC: Government Printing Office. For the population of Lakewood Club, MI: *Hammond Contemporary World Atlas*. 1971. Garden City, NY: Doubleday and Company, 1971. Population characteristics are unavailable when the population is less than 1,000.

pocketbooks. Race, according to this argument, is not the cause; the cause is really the presence of poor populations.

In order to assess the validity of this critique, I re-estimated the above analyses for the formation of cities in the 1950s and 1960s, the two analyses where race seemed to play a significant role. I included the number of poor families in the county at the beginning of the decade. And I included the interaction between the number of poor families and the corporate tax rate. If the alternative explanation were correct, the coefficients and effects of the racial composition variables would become statistically and substantively insignificant, either because the cause is really poor people (in which case the coefficients on the measures of the presence of poor people would be statistically significant and the coefficients on the race variable would become statistically insignificant) or because there is so much overlap between the presence of poor people and the presence of African-Americans that the quantitative analyses simply cannot distinguish between the two (in which case neither the racial nor the income variables would be statistically significant). I present the results of these analyses in Table 5.8; as before, I include the coefficient and robust standard error estimates in the appendix.

If anything, the result of these analyses is that the effects of race are accentuated and the effects of income are mixed when these additional variables are included. With the controls for the presence of poor populations in the 1950s, the presence of low corporate taxes and large African-American populations led to the formation of 0.94 new cities. In the earlier analyses, before I included the variables for income, this combination led citizens to form only 0.29 new cities. In the 1960s, this effect was even larger; the presence of low corporate taxes and large African-American populations led to the formation of *4.46* new cities, whereas before it led to the formation of only 0.11 new cities. This is a *huge* effect.

The presence of laws allowing annexation enhances the effect of the combination of racial composition and entrepreneurs. Where unilateral annexation was legal, the combination led citizens to form 9.16 more cities. Where annexation was legal but citizens had some defense against it, they still formed 8.05 new cities. And where annexation was illegal, the combination had little effect: 0.0004 new cities. Again, annexation efforts were able to trigger formation attempts.

The low-income variables have much smaller effects. Oddly, where entrepreneurial conditions were unsuitable, large poor populations seemed to lead to the formation of slightly more cities (0.13 in the 1950s and 0.02 in the 1960s). Where entrepreneurial conditions were favorable, large poor populations actually depressed formations: 0.03 fewer in the 1950s and 0.10 fewer in the 1960s.

This evidence suggests, then, that the operative concern here was race, and not simply the presence of low-income populations. The founders' goal, it seems, was the exclusion of African-Americans.

Table 5.8.   Municipal Creation in the 1950s and 1960s

Effect
(Mean)
(Range Over Which Evaluated)
$*p < .10$ $**p < .05$ $***p < .001$

Variable	1950s	1960s
Number of nonwhite residents interacted with corporate tax rate		
Higher taxes	−0.04***	−0.11***
Lower taxes	0.94***	4.46***
	(29)	(42.5)
	[number of nonwhite residents: 0,28]	[number of nonwhite residents: 0,36.5]
Number of families in poverty interacted with corporate tax rate		
Higher taxes	0.13**	0.02**
Lower taxes	−0.03**	−0.10**
	(20.2)	(21.7)
	[number of poor families: 0.10,9]	[number of poor families: 0.10,8]

Special Districts. In the analyses of special district formations in the 1950s, the combination of large African-American populations and developers had an effect similar to that of municipalities upon the formation of special districts. The presence of entrepreneurs seemed to dampen the negative influence of large African-American populations upon the formation of special districts. Special districts, however, do not zone. Thus, the explanation cannot be exactly the same as the explanation for the role of race in municipal incorporation. Although special districts are able to remove issues from popular politics and are not particularly representative institutions, we will see that racially exclusionary motivations are most likely not the cause of the formation of these special districts in the 1950s. Instead, the most plausible explanation here appears to be citizens' desire for low-cost housing coupled with the presence of developers who could profit from the provision of that housing.

This section, like the section on municipalities, looks first at where the special districts were formed. Then it examines the functions of these districts to illuminate the role of race in their formation. The focus is upon counties (1) with relatively large African-American populations and entrepreneurial conditions (2) where the model predicted special district formations and they actually did form.

Where Did These Districts Form? The fact that the combination of entrepreneurs and large African-American populations was associated with the formation of special districts in the 1950s could mean one of two things. On the one hand, it could mean that white citizens with racially exclusionary motivations wanted to make their politics more exclusively white and thus created fairly unrepresentative institutions to accomplish that. On the other hand, it could mean that large African-American populations pressed political demands for services effectively, and developers enabled them to acquire these services. The only places where either scenario is plausible are places where the Voting Rights Act did not take effect in the mid-1960s. These were the only counties with the potential for effective African-American political participation. For either explanation to be valid, the places (1) with real estate and financial concerns *and* (2) with large African-American populations *and* (3) where predicted formations actually occurred should not be counties where African-Americans were excluded from political participation.[5] These counties should not have been among those that were covered by Section 5 of the Voting Rights Act in the mid-1960s.

Table 5.9 presents the location of these new districts. None of these formations was in a county covered by Section 5 of the Voting Rights Act in the mid-1960s. This suggests that one of these two explanations could be accurate; we need more evidence to determine whether one explanation is more plausible than the other.

Can We Say More About Special Districts? Unlike municipalities, the Census Bureau does not collect information on the racial composition of the population governed by special districts. However, there is one potentially informative analysis remaining—an examination of the functions provided by the new special districts. Table 5.10 gives this information.

This list is helpful. The one commonality among the various places is the formation of a housing authority to provide low-cost housing to the community. This suggests that the motivations may not have been racially exclusionary. Instead, the reasons, like all of the other reasons associated with special districts, may have simply been service provision—in this case, the provision of low-cost housing. This service provision—as

Table 5.9.   Counties in Which the Models Suggest Race as an Important
Factor in the Creation of Special Districts

Counties with African-American populations larger than the mean, with entrepreneurial conditions, with local government formations, and with predicted formations of
0.50 or greater

Special Districts, 1950s

Contra Costa, CA	8 formations	7.82 predicted
New Haven, CT	2 formations	1.97 predicted
Broward, FL	2 formations	1.29 predicted

---

in many of the other cases of special district creation—redounded to the
benefit of local developers, thereby lending some power to the combination of developers and relatively large African-American populations
in the 1950s. Developers were able to dampen the negative effect of racial
composition upon special district formation.

These results suggest that citizens and entrepreneurs combined to create racially exclusionary cities in the United States in the 1950s and

Table 5.10.   Functions of the New Districts, 1950s

Contra Costa, CA
    Castle Rock Water Utility   Water utility
    Crockett Valona Sewerage
      District   Sewerage
    Housing Authority   Housing and community development
    Kensington Commission   NA
    Oakley County Water District   Water utility
    Pleasant Hill Park District   Parks and recreation
    Green Valley Park District   Parks and recreation
    Rollingwood Willard Park District   Parks and recreation
New Haven, CT
    Housing Authority   Housing and community development
    Lee Manor Association   NA
Broward, FL
    Housing Authority   Housing and community development
    Tindall Hammock Flood
      Control District   Flood control
    Citrus County Mosquito
      District   Mosquito abatement

1960s. Whites, the evidence suggests, were able to make these exclusionary politics endure even after systematic racial reasons for forming cities disappeared. They institutionalized two kinds of private values. They created governments that could ensure lower taxes for a time, and they created governments that could ensure racial exclusion.

Entrepreneurs enabled racial composition to matter in special district formation politics in a completely different way. Developers and African-Americans seem to have combined to create housing authorities in some counties in the 1950s.

The Legal Structures of Supply

> The undifferentiated citizen, whose needs the government was to serve, and whose freedom in disposing of his income was to be absolute, was visualized, not as a producer, whether lawyer or land cultivator, cleric or craftsman, physician or farrier, but entirely as a consumer of commodities and services.
>
> SIDNEY AND BEATRICE WEBB

States have influenced the formation of these new governments in two ways. First, they have determined how easy it will be to form these governments. Second, they have defined the institutions of the local governments and have delineated the process of creating these new governments. The first of these points is mundane. Where states (or the federal government) make it harder for citizens to form new local governments, they form fewer of them. Citizens find it harder to institutionalize desires for services, lower taxes, or racial exclusion in some places as a consequence. The second of these points has even larger consequences for local politics because it means that states *define* the relevant interested actors in local politics. In defining the bundle of institutions that constitute local government, states go a long way toward defining the political issues in local politics. I will discuss the more mundane point here and develop the other point in the next chapter.

As I discussed in Chapter 3, where movements to outlaw special legislation succeeded in the nineteenth century, when citizens wanted to form special districts, state legislatures had to pass enabling legislation for an entire class of districts (water districts, for example) rather than for a single district (the Plainview Water District, for example). As a consequence, states where anti-special-legislation movements succeeded have many more special district enabling laws and have general enabling laws for municipal formation. States where these movements failed tend to have very few general laws and tend to allow municipal incorporation only by special act of the legislature.

State legislatures have also influenced the formation process by (1) creating varying laws concerning annexation, (2) enabling cities to zone, (3) allowing only property owners to vote in some special district elections, (4) preventing cities from taxing their neighbors, and (5) creating varying forms of tax levy limits on local governments. Interestingly, some other things that state governments have done do not seem to matter much for the formation of new governments—allowing interlocal service agreements, enabling the initiators of district formation to be predominantly citizens (as opposed to government officials), and enacting tax rate and debt limits for local governments.

The federal government also influenced the formation process with the enactment of the Voting Rights Act. This act increased the racially and ethnically based incentives to form municipalities *and* made it more difficult to form both special districts and municipalities (as a consequence of the Section 5 preclearance requirements).

Special Districts

Table 5.11 presents the results of the analyses of special district formation. Over the thirty-seven years, the presence of more special district enabling laws consistently meant that citizens formed more special districts. In most decades, it meant citizens' forming one-third to one-half of a government more than did citizens of other counties. In the 1970s, however, enabling legislation was even more important. Where more enabling legislation was in effect, citizens formed an entire government more than did citizens of other counties.

The Voting Rights Act slowed the formation of special districts. It had its largest effect in the decade in which it was enacted. Citizens in preclearance-covered counties formed about two-thirds of a special district fewer than did citizens of other counties in the 1960s. After the 1960s, the effect of the Voting Rights Act was smaller. Citizens formed one-quarter of a special district government fewer in covered counties than in counties without Section 5 coverage.

Table 5.11. Special Districts and Supply

Effect
(Mean of X)
[Range Over Which Evaluated]

Variable	1950s	1960s	1970s	1980s
Number of special district general enabling laws	0.33*** (8) [3,13]	0.45*** (10) [4,15]	1.06*** (11) [5,17]	0.37*** (13) [7,19]
Voting Rights Act coverage		-0.68*** (0.20) [0,1]	-0.21* (0.30) [0,1]	-0.24** (0.30) [0,1]

Municipalities

The legal structures of supply had a smaller influence on the formation of municipalities than on the formation of special districts (Table 5.12). In the 1950s and the 1980s, citizens in counties where municipalities could be formed only by special act of the legislature formed slightly fewer cities than did citizens of other counties. The Voting Rights Act mattered only in the 1980s, when it seems to have had a slightly bigger influence upon the demand than upon the supply of municipalities. Where the Section 5 preclearance requirements were in effect, citizens formed a tiny 0.004 more cities than they did elsewhere. And in the 1960s and 1970s, the presence of a larger number of general enabling laws for special districts meant the formation of more cities.

At first reading, this last result is puzzling: Where the supply of the alternative form of government was greater, citizens formed more cities. One possible reason for this result is simply that where special districts were more available, cities were able to provide even fewer services and thus could be even cheaper forms of government. Thus, instead of indicating the availability of a potentially easier-to-form alternative source of services, the presence of more general enabling legislation for special districts may simply indicate that new cities are even cheaper forms of government than they are elsewhere.[6] This result lends more credence to the argument presented earlier that cities were rarely formed for service reasons after the 1950s. If they had been formed for service reasons, special districts would have been a substitute for rather than a complement of new cities.

Table 5.12.   Municipalities and Supply

Effect
(Mean of X)
[Range Over Which Evaluated]

Variable	1950s	1960s	1970s	1980s
Special act of the legislature required for incorporation	**−0.08***			**−0.006***
	(0.07)			(0.13)
	[0,1]			[0,1]
Number of special district enabling laws		**0.05**	**0.03*	
		(10)	(11)	
		[4,15]	[5,17]	
Voting Rights Act coverage				**0.004**
				(0.30)
				[0,1]

Small Groups, Entrepreneurs, and the Enabling of Collective Action

One maine end of towns is to settle Manufactures.

EDWARD RANDOLPH,
Virginia General Assembly, 1692[7]

Political entrepreneurs and small groups enabled some forces to succeed and allowed some forces to wither in the formation of local governments. These groups and entrepreneurs—developers and manufacturers—have made special districts providers of infrastructure for new developments and municipalities providers of walls against higher taxes and against African-Americans. The consequences are that tax motivations won in formation politics over the entire thirty-seven years and that racial motivations had overwhelming power in the formation of U.S. cities in the 1950s and 1960s.

Special Districts

Table 5.13 presents the effects of developers in special district formation politics over these thirty-seven years. In the 1950s, the results suggest, developers influenced the formation of special districts only when they combined with relatively large African-American populations.

Table 5.13.   Special Districts and Entrepreneurs

Effect
(Mean of *X*)
[Range Over Which Evaluated]

Variable	1950s	1960s	1970s	1980s
Number of nonwhite residents interacted with the log of the number of real estate and financial firms				
Few entrepreneurs	−.74**			
More entrepreneurs	−.57**			
	(23.6)			
	[in racial composition: 0,28]			
Number of developers		7.34***		
		(0.75)		
		[1,6]		
Number of developers interacted with median family income				
Few developers		−0.19***		
More developers		−0.19***		
		(4132)		
		[in income: $2,845, $5,406]		
Annexation allowed, unilateral			−1.87***	−.40**
			(0.12)	(0.12)
			[0,1]	[0,1]
Annexation allowed; citizens to be annexed have at least one channel of defense			−1.84***	−.30*
			(0.80)	(0.80)
			[0,1]	[0,1]

Developers were able to weaken the dampening effect of large African-American populations upon the formation of special districts in the 1950s. This makes sense for two reasons. First, the 1950s were the last decade in which developers were able to rely heavily upon annexation and municipal financing of infrastructure, arguably easier paths to costless land improvement than the formation of a new government. By the 1960s—

with the increasing expensiveness of local government—this was no longer true. Second, in the 1950s, developers could profit by the creation of local housing authorities, which could furnish low-cost housing built by these same developers.

In the late 1960s, developers continued to matter in special district formation politics. Developers were beginning to face funding limitations in areas where income was lower. Where median family income was lower, there were more formations. The effect, however, was modest. The interaction with the number of developers did not alter the effect of median income. But entrepreneurs alone had quite a large effect. Where there were six developers, *seven and one-third* more special districts formed than where there were no developers.

In the 1970s, more special districts formed where developers did not have any other alternatives for public funding of infrastructure. Where annexation was not allowed, developers formed more special districts than they did either where annexation could be accomplished unilaterally or where citizens had some defense against annexation.

This interpretation is bolstered by the effects of the previously mentioned tax limits in the presence of the various annexation laws. Where annexation was illegal—where developers had no chance of having services provided to new developments by existing cities—the presence of tax levy limits that further constrained the sources of infrastructure funding for new developments meant 1.88 new special districts. Where annexation was legal, the presence of tax levy limits had a much smaller effect: They led to the formation of about one-half of a special district.

In the 1980s, developers mattered in much the same way that they mattered in the 1970s, although the effects were somewhat smaller. Where annexation was allowed, there were fewer formations than where annexation was illegal. Where, then, developers had greater difficulty in using existing cities to provide their new developments with infrastructure, they continued to turn to the formation of special districts.

Municipalities

Tables 5.14.1 and 5.14.2 present the effects of manufacturers in city formation politics. The effects here are quite large.

Entrepreneurs influenced the formation of municipalities. Where manufacturers existed to undertake these entrepreneurial activities, there was a small increase in the number of municipal incorporations. Table

Table 5.14.1. Municipalities and Entrepreneurs

Effect
(Mean of *X*)
[Range Over Which Evaluated]

Variable	1950s	1960s	1970s	1980s
Corporate tax rate interacted with median family income				
Higher taxes	**0.004**			
Lower taxes	**0.02**			
	($14,037)			
	[in income:			
	$1,495,			
	$3,093]			
Corporate tax rate interacted with number of nonwhite residents				
Higher taxes	**−0.08*****	**−0.08*****		
Lower taxes	**0.29*****	**0.11*****		
	(29)	(42.5)		
	[in racial	[in racial		
	composition:	composition:		
	0,28]	0,36.5]		
Whether a tax levy limit is in effect	**−0.05*****		**−0.05*****	
	(0.02)		(0.02)	
	[0,1]		[0,1]	
Whether there are manufacturers in the county	**0.05*****	**0.13*****	**0.05*****	**0.002*****
	(0.98)	(0.98)	(0.98)	(0.97)
	[0,1]	[0,1]	[0,1]	[0,1]

5.15 demonstrates this effect in the 1950s. With one exception, where there were no manufacturers, there were no municipal incorporations. And where manufacturers could acquire tax limits from other sources—where there were tax levy limits—there were about 0.05 fewer municipalties formed than elsewhere.

When manufacturers combined with relatively well-off populations in the 1950s, the result was one-twentieth of a new city. Without manufacturers with tax incentives to create new cities, the median income of the county's residents did not matter in municipal formation politics.

When manufacturers had tax incentives to create cities, they enabled

Table 5.14.2.   Municipalities and Entrepreneurs

Effect
(Mean of X)
[Range Over Which Evaluated]

Variable	1950s	1960s	1970s	1980s
Corporate tax rate interacted with the log of the number of manufacturers				
Higher taxes			0.01***	
Lower taxes			0.10***	
			(23)	
			[in log of manufacturers: 2,5]	
Corporate tax rate interacted with the number of Latino residents				
Higher taxes				.0007***
Lower taxes				−.001***
				(41)
				[in Latino population: 0,30]

racial composition to encourage the formation of new cities. Where there was a relatively large African-American population and where there were low state corporate taxes, *one-quarter* of a new city formed in the 1950s. As I discussed in the section on racial effects, these results seem most consistent with the argument that manufacturers enabled white citizens to create racially exclusive cities in areas with large African-American populations. These racial effects continued into the 1960s. They disappeared in the 1970s and 1980s.

The presence of manufacturers continued to encourage the formation of cities throughout the entire study period. Tables 5.16, 5.17, and 5.18 reinforce this result. In general, cities formed only where there were manufacturing firms to help out. In the 1970s, tax levy limits again effectively diminished manufacturers' tax incentives for forming new cities. In the 1970s, the presence—alone—of manufacturers with incentives

Table 5.15. Manufacturer Presence and Incorporation, 1950s, in the 200 Counties

		Whether There Were Two Manufacturers in the County, 1950	
		No	*Yes*
Number of municipal formations	0	13	158
1950–59	1	1	20
	2	0	4
	4	0	4
	7	0	2

Table 5.16. Manufacturer Presence and Incorporation, 1960s, in the 200 Counties

		Whether There Was a Manufacturer in the County, 1960	
		No	*Yes*
Number of municipal formations	0	5	152
1960–69	1	0	30
	2	0	7
	3	0	3
	4	1	1
	8	0	1

Table 5.17. Manufacturer Presence and Incorporation, 1970s, in the 200 Counties

		Whether There Was a Manufacturer in the County, 1970	
		No	*Yes*
Number of municipal formations	0	4	173
1970–79	1	0	19
	2	0	2
	3	0	1
	4	1	0

Table 5.18. Manufacturer Presence and Incorporation, 1980s, in the 200 Counties

		Whether There Was a Manufacturer in the County, 1980	
Number of municipal formations,		*No*	*Yes*
1980–87	0	7	182
	1	0	10
	2	0	1

to form cities meant the creation of one-tenth of a new city in some counties.

In addition to these results, the strength of tax reasons for forming cities—as discussed earlier—beginning in the 1960s and continuing throughout the 1980s is a strong suggestion of the importance of entrepreneurs. The desire to create a lower-tax enclave is the single common motivation for citizens and entrepeneurs.

Other Supporting Evidence

The argument that businesses are interested enough in the structure of local government to shoulder municipal incorporation movements is supported by the results of another study of local politics that examines local politics in the 1960s. This study is Matthew Crenson's *The Un-Politics of Air Pollution*, which concerns the power that businesses can have in local politics as a consequence of their presence alone. According to Crenson, where industry is powerful, air pollution is not an issue on the agenda of local politics. Quite significantly, the issue that correlates *most highly* with the presence or absence of air pollution on the local political agenda (higher even than water pollution—see Tables 5.19 and 5.20) is local government consolidation.[8] Government consolidation means the consolidation of the many distinct tax enclaves that I have argued businesses help create. It means the destruction of legal walls against higher taxes. That the absence of air pollution from the local political agenda correlates most highly with the absence of government consolidation illuminates and strengthens Crenson's own argument. He was not able to explain this correlation with government consolidation. He said of the

Table 5.19. The Prominence of the Air Pollution Problem and the Salience of Other Civic Problems, Controlling for Suspended Particulate Level

Civic Problem	Association with the Prominence of Air Pollution as a Civic Problem
Government consolidation	+.42
Water pollution and sewage disposal	+.39
Mass transit	+.25
Crime, police, and fire protection	+.20
Race relations	+.17
Loss of taxpaying residents	+.14
Municipal revenue and taxes	+.07
Public education	+.06
Recreation and parks	+.03
Unemployment	−.01
Wages and working conditions of public employees	−.02
Central business district renewal	−.03
Building and zoning codes	−.05
Traffic, streets, and parking	−.06
Housing	−.09
General conflict and public mistrust	−.11
Poverty and welfare	−.15
Business and industrial development	−.37

Source: Matthew A. Crenson. 1971. *The Un-Politics of Air Pollution*. Baltimore: Johns Hopkins University Press, p. 164.

Table 5.20. Intercorrelation Among Selected Items on Political Agendas

Variable	Government Consolidation
Air pollution	+.34
Water pollution	+.39
Crime	−.06
Mass transit	−.03
Race relations	−.06

Source: Matthew A. Crenson. 1971. *The Un-Politics of Air Pollution*. Baltimore: Johns Hopkins University Press, p. 164.

correlation: "There is no obvious reason, for example, why local concern for mass transit or government reorganization should interfere with a community's effort to make itself attractive to business and industry."[9] There is a reason, a reason suggested by the argument presented here. Government consolidations make local government cost more for businesses—or, at least, businesses seem to think they do.

Crenson argued that where industry is strong, air pollution is *not* on the agenda of local politics. His results show as well that where industry is strong, government consolidation is also *not* on the agenda of local politics. Without the results offered here, this is a puzzling finding. However, if, as I have suggested, businesses support the creation of new cities to keep themselves walled off from older cities with higher taxes, these same businesses should oppose strongly any effort to remove those walls through government consolidation. Crenson's results make sense in light of the argument presented here and, in fact, provide additional evidence to support that argument. It is the separation of the new government from citizens with service needs that allows these governments to operate so inexpensively. Metropolitan consolidation is the opposite of this separation.

A Note on Whether Businesses Get What They Want When They Form Municipalities

If businesses form cities in order to acquire lower tax burdens, we would expect these newly formed city tax havens to be magnets for other businesses. This is overwhelmingly the case. If we regress the number of new manufacturing establishments started in a county from 1960 to 1970 upon the number of new municipalities formed in the county in the 1950s, we get the results presented in Table 5.21.

I included both the state corporate tax rate in 1960 and the number of new special districts in the 1950s in my original specification. These two variables had no statistically significant effect, and omitting them did not induce omitted variable bias.

Counties where one new municipality formed, then, acquired 32 more new manufacturing establishments in the following decade than did counties where no new municipalities formed. The effect increases linearly; where two municipalities formed, there were 64 new manufacturing establishments. This is a *huge* effect, with huge consequences for the

Table 5.21. New Manufacturing Establishments
in the 1960s, Ordinary Least Squares

Variable	Coefficient Estimate	Robust Standard Error
Number of new municipalities, 1950–60	32.37	13.90
Intercept	−1.15	2.64

Number of observations: 198
Adjusted *R*-squared: 0.30

local economy. It seems that, from the perspective of businesspersons deciding where to locate manufacturing establishments, new municipalities look particularly nice.

This effect increases if we look at the number of new manufacturers in the 1970s regressed upon the number of new municipalities formed in the 1960s. I report the results of this analysis in Table 5.22.

For every new municipality incorporated in a county in the 1960s, *48* new manufacturing establishments sprang up in the 1970s. Again, this is a huge effect. Counties with no municipal creations in the 1960s lost about one and a half manufacturing establishments in the 1970s. Counties with one municipal creation in the 1960s gained 46.27 (47.66 − 1.39) manufacturing establishments. Counties with two municipal creations in the 1960s gained *93.93* manufacturing establishments in the next decade. With these kinds of effects, manufacturing establishments seem to get what they want when they sustain a municipal formation effort.

These results suggest that developers and manufacturers have systematically structured the creation of local governments in America for the thirty-seven years between 1950 and 1987. When citizens had developers' or manufacturers' support for the creation of a new local government, they largely succeeded in their efforts. Without this support, they generally failed. The consequence is that new special districts were created when they could provide infrastructure (e.g., sewerage systems and new roads) that would redound to the benefit of developers. By the same token, new cities were formed when they achieved lower taxes for busi-

Table 5.22.   New Manufacturing Establishments
in the 1970s, Ordinary Least Squares

Variable	Coefficient Estimate	Robust Standard Error
Number of new municipalities, 1960–70	47.66	13.62
Intercept	−1.39	5.08

Number of observations: 194
Adjusted *R*-squared: 0.31

nesses (and manufacturers, in particular). Because special districts could easily be created by small groups (composed even of one single developer), new special districts embodied the values of these developers. Municipalities, on the other hand, generally required entrepreneurial efforts. The consequence is that new cities embody two sets of values—those of entrepreneurs and those of larger groups of citizens.

6

The Meaning of Limits

My fundamental contention is that the city is a corporation; that as a city it has nothing whatever to do with general political interest . . . . The questions in a city are not political questions. They have reference to the laying out of streets [and such matters]. The work of a city [is] . . . the creation and control of city property.
—ANDREW D. WHITE, 1890[1]

Citizens create local governments for many reasons. These reasons change as the institutions themselves evolve through accretion, innovation, and obsolescence and as the historical context in which these institutions exist changes. White citizens have created local governments to provide services, to build exclusionary walls against lower classes and African-Americans, and to insulate themselves from the taxes and the problems of existing and older cities. These citizens have been assisted in this effort by organizations and individuals who have the money, the organization, and the interest to channel these citizen desires and to make them succeed in risk-filled, expensive politics. In recent years, these organizations and individuals have been manufacturers that have wanted cities to create low-tax havens and developers who have wanted special districts to improve property and create developer profits at public expense.

These governments could be used by these various individuals and groups because American local governments have substantial power to define citizenship, to take and assemble land through eminent domain, and to tax, issue debt, and spend money. It is precisely for these reasons that citizens, small groups, and entrepreneurs have believed them useful.

That citizens have continued to form cities and special districts over the past 350 years informs us about local political institutions, local politics itself, and the place of those institutions and politics within the American political system. It points to the ways in which those institutions have changed. It illuminates activities of both the institutions and those who sought to create them. As a consequence, it provides us with a clearer picture of the place of local politics in America.

In this concluding chapter, I will first draw together strands from several chapters (2, 3, and 5) to outline broadly the changing institutions of local politics and their changing place in American politics. I will then examine how understanding the creation of these governments can change our view of local politics. Finally, I will turn to the normative implications of the study.

Empirical Results

Local government has been defined and redefined over the course of American history. It was first a place of limited autonomy that provided a few services such as fence viewing and tending of the indigenous poor. More significantly, local government defined citizenship through inspection of potential residents, and the simple existence of local government increased land values. To be sure, local government could build another kind of wall around itself to create actual defensive fortifications. Citizens created new governments to provide some of these services, to increase the value of land, and to exclude unwanted others from relatively homogeneous communities. Those excluded, in particular, were those who threatened to become chargeable to the town. Persons who had already been defined as citizens of the town were not keen on extending citizenship to those who would enlarge their tax bills or create social disorder. The walls—visible and invisible—made local government valuable. The walls defined the nature of services and the type of exclusion possible, and in that way provided some limited definition and insurance of property rights.

In the nineteenth century, local government underwent a profound transformation. The nature of its autonomy was redefined. Technological developments and market failures led to public provision of more expensive services by cities and by special districts. These governments' bond-issuing powers were extended, exploited, and refined from the 1837 panic on, largely through the efforts of the railroads. These governments' autonomy was in a state of flux during most of the century—

with legal scholars, politicians with progressive ambition, political bosses, and business reformers each seeking to provide a particular definition of the scope and character of that autonomy. Their autonomy, by and large, was settled in a number of states by the end of the century with the compromise composed of Dillon's rule, home rule, and the abolition of special legislation. By the end of the century, a space had been carved out for local autonomy.

Over the course of the nineteenth century, cities were used to provide services, to increase land values and speculators' profits dramatically, and to improve the local business climate. Special districts were beginning to be more widely employed to exert eminent domain and provide extensive services in the face of market failures and in the context of the invention of revenue bonds. Less attention seems to have been paid to local governments' capacity to define citizenship through exclusion in the nineteenth century, although defensive incorporation of suburbs was invented during this century, commercial interests had Memphis abolished when its politics became too inclusive, and Connecticut devised the idea of poll taxes and literacy tests.[2] Citizens had to rely upon other sets of rules—restrictive deed covenants, for example—to exclude.

The place for local autonomy carved out in the nineteenth century became crucial to cities' powers to define citizenship in the twentieth century, with the importation and redefinition of zoning in 1916 and with the outlawing of race-restrictive deed covenants in 1948. In addition, with the organization of the professions of developers and manufacturers and the further nationalization of business location decisions, special districts became the main providers of land improvement, while cities became the main providers of exclusion of both races and classes. And developers were considering special districts as alternative financing mechanisms. To be sure, influential citizens still wanted some services, but this trend would not last throughout the 1960s.

In the 1950s, citizens and entrepreneurs created special districts to provide services and cities to provide services, racial exclusion, and business tax havens. In the 1960s, citizens and developers continued to create special districts to provide services and improve land. But new cities changed in character. While they were still service providers, they were also (and perhaps more importantly) providers of tax limitations and racial exclusion. And in the 1970s, cities were formed exclusively to provide tax limitation. By the 1980s, this tax-revolt/tax-base politics, which had become a strong force in the 1960s, became the dominant force in the creation of local political institutions. Citizens no longer formed even special districts to provide services; only developers did.

During the same period, the federal government restricted the capacity of states and cities to define citizenship along racial lines. Before the reforms of the mid-1960s, states and cities could block African-Americans from institutional forms of politics, without regard to their residence. Residence—even of American citizens—did not mean citizenship in cities and states. (It still does not mean citizenship in special districts.) In the 1970s, these reforms, combined with increasing African-American affluence, meant the eradication of systematic racial reasons for city creation. Nevertheless, the boundaries created by citizens and entrepreneurs can still effectively segregate races to the extent that African-Americans continue to have low incomes. The space created for local autonomy thus gives these cities' boundaries racial meaning in school, housing, and redistributive politics as long as this correlation between income and race exists.

Implications

State legislatures and the federal government have at various points in history altered the powers of local governments to issue debt and define citizenship, and states in particular have defined and redefined the space for local autonomy. In that way, these other levels of government have changed the meaning of cities, in particular, and of local politics more generally. They have changed the character of groups and individuals who have both an *interest* in local politics and the *resources* to act on that interest.

Institutional Definitions

Throughout, the most important institutions of the city and of the special district government have not been solely the institutions (in the narrow sense) of governance. That is, they have not consisted solely of mechanisms such as political machines or commission governments or open meetings, although these institutions have clearly been important.[3] The relevant institutions have also been the institutions (in the broader sense) that constituted these goverments—that is, institutions such as state and federal laws that define the powers of local government and therefore define the ways in which citizens employed these governments to achieve their own private ends. By and large, these institutions—these parameters in which local government operates—define the issues of local politics to be development, taxes, services, and exclusion.

Not surprisingly, those with the interest and the resources are most able to use these institutions to achieve their own private ends. Also not surprisingly, the interested and resource rich are developers, businesses, and well-to-do homeowners' associations.

We can see the import of these powers and of their definition and redefinition if we think, for example, about local politics in the late nineteenth century. These politics embodied the limits of the powers noted above. Local governments in the late nineteenth century were at the one point in American history when their powers to define citizenship were weak—no zoning, no resident inspection. Creating a local government at that time could provide access to powers of eminent domain and bond financing, and people could leave cities if they didn't like their neighbors, but they could not keep others out of their own cities. Erie notes the beginning of the exodus of the middle class from big cities as taxes were increasing.[4] But local politics in the nineteenth century still had the potential to be redistributive. The wealthy could not create their own local governments through exclusionary zoning because zoning simply did not exist. Reliance upon deed covenants meant that citizens could make their own neighborhoods somewhat more homogeneous than would have been achieved by chance. But the mechanism was imperfect and required the employment of extensive small-scale organization. So city boundaries meant different things in the 1890s than in the late twentieth century; in particular, they did not necessarily signify rigidly demarcated classes and races.

Institutional Constraints

This change in the meaning of city boundaries affects our theoretical understanding of local politics. Peterson, for example, argues that cities have severely restricted capabilities to engage in meaningfully redistributive politics.[5] Criticizing this view, Erie notes that the late-nineteenth-century cities he studied actually performed more redistribution than did the federal government of that era.[6] Erie points to the lack of mobility of businesses as the reason cities could engage in redistributive politics in the 1890s. This is an important point, one that Peterson himself makes,[7] but there is an additional vital reason why Peterson's argument is insightful for the era in which he writes and an important reason why local politics was different in the late nineteenth century. Cities can define their residents relatively effectively in the late twentieth century; city limits can mean boundaries between classes and races in ways that they could not in the late nineteenth century. This fact accentuates the difficulties of redistribution that Peterson notes. Not only are cities constrained by the logic of federalism to minimize their social service expenditures, but if cities play their boundary cards right, they may not even have citizens in need of social services. Some places, then, can have lower taxes than other places, and thus provide better business climates, as well as increase pressure on cities with poor residents to keep their own taxes low and their social services minimal. Moreover, this study has documented an additional constraint: If businesses do not find existing city policies agreeable, not only can they leave, but they can also create their own cities or special districts with their own boundaries and their own definitions of citizenship.

Institutional Politics

Local politics has often been considered an important but restrained category of action. Once the structural and economic features of local politics are in place, local politics appear to consist primarily of coalition building around these existing structures and economies.[8] The perspective developed here adds an important dimension to these politics— the fight over boundaries and over access to the institutions of local government.[9] Sometimes this politics is played out in cities—with efforts to zone and rezone and float bonds—and sometimes this politics is played out in state legislatures, in the courts, and in Congress. Again, many of these fights are not so much about the narrower institutions of local governance as about access to the powers of local government. These fights ultimately define the ways in which resource-rich American citizens will use local governments. The resource poor generally lose in fights over access to these broader institutions.[10]

Regardless of who wins and who loses, it should be clear that we miss much of the fight when we focus only on cities. Local government is a collection of governments.[11] When we discuss who has power in local politics, how much money is spent in local politics, and whether local politics is participatory or representative, for example, we provide distorted answers if our focus is solely upon cities. While we focus upon cities, the politics spill into the arena of special districts, and our focus then becomes a smaller and smaller part of what is really happening in American local government.

Development politics, in particular, are clearly not mostly fights within cities. They are played out largely in the realm of special districts.[12] These special districts lower the risk and the cost of development immensely, arguably encouraging more speculative efforts where special districts are easier to form. Developers clearly win more easily in this realm; often they create the realm precisely for that reason.

Realms other than development are becoming the preserve of special districts. Service politics are moving in the direction of special districts. Housing politics have been special district politics since the 1930s.[13]

Part of the contribution of this work, then, is that it illuminates the structural characteristics of the content of local politics and helps us better understand why certain types of controversies appear and reappear in our analyses of local politics. These recurrent features are those embodied in the structure of the institutions—taxes and tax bases, eminent domain, infrastructure provision and land improvement, zoning, services, and race. If we want local politics to be about different issues, then we must redefine the institutions—change the parameters in which local government operates—which will, in turn, redefine the character of the interested parties. Changing the narrower institutions of governance—opening meetings to the public and abolishing political parties in local politics, for example—alters local politics and can make those politics more or less inclusive.[14] However, changing the narrower institutions of governance alone does not change who wins in city politics. As long as the rewards for controlling local government remain the same, the same people will have an interest in gaining that control. The agenda may change somewhat. In the end, however, the new politics probably look a lot like the old politics because the institutions that constitute the government in the first place remain untouched.

Instead, this work suggests that the two changes that *would* make a difference are (1) changing the institutions themselves and (2) fostering more citizen organization to overcome the influence of the institutions. In the first instance, one would (with great difficulty) change the powers of the institutions to make them less useful for guaranteeing lower taxes, ensuring exclusion, and (perhaps) providing infrastructure. Such changes would make developers and manufacturers less interested in acquiring these powers. Importantly, however, one might also change the nature of incentives for development, for good or ill. In the second instance, those in government mobilize and give resources to those with other interests in city politics.[15] Or the citizenry has abundant resources and organization that combine with other interests in city politics (in college towns, for example) to reduce the influence of the institutions on the politics.[16]

Private Values in Public Institutions

How does the portrait of local politics I have presented change our understanding of the role of local government in the American polity? Political philosophers have often idealized local politics and pictured local institutions as natural, benevolent institutions that are the perfect training ground for democratic citizens. The endogeneity of these local institutions, however, illuminates the fact that they are often created for reasons that often impair their ability to be democratic training grounds. Moreover, special districts function to discourage participation because, as noted in Chapter 1, the information costs associated with learning even the names of the districts that govern a location are prohibitive. Thus, while citizens may have enough information to decide whether to live in Plainville or in Arborview, rarely will they have enough information to locate the areas where special district governments overlap to provide their desired bundle of services.

The collective action problems inherent in efforts to form special districts and cities are solved in three ways that have important implications for democratic politics. First, they are solved by small groups. Special districts tend to be formed, for example, by a single developer; there are cases in which cities have been formed by small groups of manufacturers. The consequence of this collective action solution is that developers' and manufacturers' preferences are institutionalized, without compromise. Local government becomes government by this set of private values.

Second, when the collective action problem is solved by reliance upon an existing organization, the new government embodies the values of that organization. Thus, when wealthy homeowners' associations with the desire to exclude are used to form cities, the new cities are exclusionary.

Finally, when entrepreneurs solve the collective action problem (as in the creation of many cities), the result is a government that embodies two sets of values—those of the entrepreneur and those of the citizens necessary to the formation effort. Unfortunately for assumptions of those who idealize local politics, even in these cases, the values embedded in the new institutions tend to be exclusionary instead of participatory.

Most likely these institutions can train citizens in the skills of politics—how to contact, how to petition, how to vote. But (1) the resulting content of politics will be limited by the structural and institutional features of local politics and (2) the possibilities for transformative public discussion within the local arena are slim. Americans have discovered in local institutions effective barriers to racial and economic integration. Living within particular city boundaries means that schools will not be integrated, that neighborhoods will not be integrated, that offensive industry will not be apparent, and that taxes will not be higher. It also means that the problems of people in other—even, and especially, neighboring—cities will be considered irrelevant to local politics.

The way in which Americans have constructed local autonomy means that we have created a space in American politics where race and class are embedded in boundaries. Because municipal boundaries can be boundaries between races and classes, boundaries that reinforce homogeneity, the possibilities for transformative public discussion in local politics are severely limited.[17]

Moreover, the space we have created for local political autonomy means that we allow local boundaries to define citizenship, and we allow that definition of citizenship to carry weight in American politics. Boundaries, and the import we give to them, can thus legally impede desegregation efforts, halt efforts at redistribution, and restrict access to services. Clearly, these boundaries do not eradicate local politics. But they do restrict the possibilities of that politics both in new cities that draw the boundaries and in old cities whose problems are accentuated by them.

Americans have also created a realm of particularly unaccountable and unrepresentative politics that has attendant benefits and problems. The benefits of special districts are that they can fund and provide services and infrastructure; they are able to get things done in a fragmented American polity. The difficulties are two: They do this while no one watches except interested developers, and they are gradually becoming the realm where much of the substance of local politics happens. Thus local politics becomes quiet, not necessarily through the consensus that the earlier studies of suburbia noted, but rather through the invisibility of special district politics.

APPENDIX A

Examples and an Outline of the Formal Procedures for Creating Cities and Special Districts

Special Districts

Table A.1 provides examples of some of the larger special districts in the sample of counties I examine in Chapter 5.

Table A.1. Examples of Some Larger Special Districts

CONTRA COSTA, CA

    Central Contra Costa Sanitary District
    Central Contra Costa Transit Authority
    Contra Costa County Housing Authority
    Contra Costa County Municipal Risk Management Authority
    Contra Costa County Water District
    Mount Diablo Hospital District
    Richmond Housing Authority
    San Ramon Valley Fire Protection District
    West Contra Costa County Hospital District
    West Contra Costa Sanitation District

SANTA CRUZ, CA

    Santa Cruz Metropolitan Transit District
    Santa Cruz Port District

SHASTA, CA

Shasta Dam Area Public Utility District
Shasta-Trinity Schools Insurance Group

SUTTER, CA

Oswald Water District
South Sutter Water District

VENTURA, CA

Calleguas Municipal Water District
Casitas Municipal Water District
Conejo Recreational Park District
Oxnard Harbor District
San Buenaventura City Housing Authority
San Buenaventura-Covina Housing Finance Agency
United Water Conservation District
Ventura County Schools Self-Funding Authority

NEW HAVEN, CT

New Haven Housing Authority
South Central Connecticut Regional Water Authority
Waterbury Housing Authority

BROWARD, FL

Broward County Housing Authority
Coral Springs Improvement District
Fort Lauderdale Housing Authority
Indian Trace Community Development District
North Broward Hospital District
Port Everglades Authority
South Broward Hospital District

HERNANDO, FL

Southwest Florida Water Management District

BALDWIN, GA

Baldwin County Hospital Authority

COFFEE, GA

Coffee County Hospital Authority

HALL, GA

Hall County Hospital Authority
Oakwood Housing Authority

120

Table A.1. (*Continued*)

WHITFIELD, GA

Dalton-Whitfield County Hospital Authority

PORTER, IN

Jackson-Liberty School Building Commission

BALTIMORE CITY, MD

Baltimore City Housing Authority
Northeast Maryland Waste Disposal Authority

BARNSTABLE, MA

Falmouth Housing Authority

MUSKEGON, MI

Muskegon County Wastewater Management System

CHISAGO, MN

Chisago Lakes Hospital District

ALCORN, MS

Tennessee Valley Regional Housing Authority

SILVER BOW, MT

Butte Housing Authority

MIDDLESEX, NJ

Middlesex County Industrial Pollution Control Financing Authority
Middlesex County Utilities Authority
Monroe Township Municipal Utilities Authority
Old Bridge Municipal Utilities Authority

PASSAIC, NJ

Passaic Valley Water Commission
Paterson Housing Authority

WAKE, NC

Eastern North Carolina Municipal Power Agency
North Carolina Municipal Power Agency
Raleigh Housing Authority
Raleigh-Durham Airport Authority

BLAIR, PA

Altoona Area School District Authority
Altoona City Authority
Blair County Hospital Authority

Table A.1. (*Continued*)

LEBANON, PA

Lebanon County Industrial Development Authority

WESTMORELAND, PA

Latrobe Borough Industrial Development Authority
Westmoreland County Housing Authority
Westmoreland County Industrial Development Authority
Westmoreland County Municipal Authority

NEWPORT, RI

Newport Housing Authority

HUMPHREYS, TN

Humphreys County Utility District

EL PASO, TX

El Paso Housing Authority

HARRISON, TX

East Texas Housing Finance Corporation

WEBER, UT

Weber Basin Water Conservancy District

DOUGLAS, WA

Douglas County Public Utility District 1

GRANT, WA

Grant County Public Hospital District 1
Grant County Public Hospital District 2
Grant County Public Utility District 2
Quincy-Columbia Basin Irrigation District

MASON, WA

Mason County Public Hospital District 1
Mason County Public Utility District 3

CAMPBELL, WY

Campbell County Hospital District

Special district enabling laws are generally passed in the state legislature. Depending upon the type of district and upon the state, a particular state may or may not have a general enabling law. When the state does have an enabling law, it contains the process for the creation of the district. For example, the law might require a petition to the county by the landowners, and then the county makes the decision by resolution; or the state may require that there be a hearing and a referendum. Some states, like Georgia and Virginia, have very few general enabling laws, whereas states like California and Illinois have many general enabling laws. In 1982 states ranged from having one enabling law to having twenty-seven; the mean is about twelve. Without general enabling laws, the individuals who wish to create a district must develop the idea from the ground up and then have the local state representative propose the formation of a new special district to the state legislature. In the 1950s, that proposal generally passed unopposed.[1] There are, however, examples of opposition to the formation of new districts.[2]

On average, states have about 11 special districts created by special act; in 1982, the number of these special districts ranged from none to 124. Some states also allow municipalities, counties, and state agencies to authorize new special districts. On average, about 30% of a state's district enabling laws allow other governments to form special districts. Forming a special district is expensive. One study finds that special district formation costs range from $5,000 to $75,000 in Arizona.[3]

Some states are becoming more restrictive with respect to the formation of local governments in an effort to slow the proliferation of these governments. Colorado now requires that petitioners for a new district demonstrate that there is not already adequate service to the area in question and that annexation would not provide adequate service. Florida in 1982 began prohibiting the creation of special districts through special acts of the legislature. Arizona recently banned the formation of special district governments until new laws are passed that would alter the formation procedures. California, Nevada, New Mexico, Oregon, and Washington have agencies that have been set up, in part, to control special district government formation.[4] Eighteen states have state advisory commissions on intergovernmental relations.[5]

Municipalities

In most states there is a general incorporation law for municipalities. As Martin notes:

Generally, the first step under a general incorporation law is to request incorporation by filing a petition with the designated agency. The petition must contain such things as the proposed boundary, the corporate name, and the signatures of a stated percentage of the area's residents. Following public notice of the petition for incorporation being officially filed and accepted, and a designated length of time to allow for objections to be filed, an election or a hearing, or both, may be required to determine whether the area will be allowed to incorporate.[6]

Some states use special charters to enable incorporation.

Whether they employ general laws or special charters, all states allow the establishment of a new municipality only "at the request or with the consent of the inhabitants."[7] Various groups of people may be allowed to begin the incorporation procedure. These individuals are "(1) a resident of the area, (2) an elector (a resident who is registered to vote), (3) an owner of real property, and (4) an elector/real property owner."[8]

These governments take a range of forms: 70% have mayor-council governments; 13% have council-manager governments; 2% have the commission form of government; 2.5% have other forms of government—town meeting, representative town meeting, or some combination of these forms.[9]

APPENDIX B

Measurement

The solution to the collective action problem in the case of special district formation is clearly measurable—simply the number of real estate developers in a county at the beginning of a decade. There are three other indicators of incentives for developer involvement in the formation of special districts: (1) whether annexation is legal and citizens have no way to stop their proposed annexation, (2) whether annexation is legal but citizens have ways to stop annexation, and (3) the median family income of the residents of the county. As some of the developers in the case studies argued, developers can acquire funding for land improvement from two sources other than themselves. They can annex the area they want to improve to an existing city *or* they can acquire a special district. When annexation is impossible, developers turn more insistently to forming special districts. The coefficients for the annexation variables (variables that indicate various ways in which annexation is legal) should thus be negative. The third variable—median family income—addresses a similar concern: a small tax base to fund the infrastructure desired by the developer. Since special districts circumvent voters and, in a sense, tax bases, we would expect developers to form more special districts where tax bases are smaller.

The measure of entrepreneurs in the case of municipalities is less obvious. More developers mean more special districts. More manufacturers do not seem to call for more municipalities; one municipality is enough. Moreover, it is not always cheaper to underwrite a formation attempt than it is to move. Particularly when state corporate taxes are relatively onerous, it might be less expensive to move than it would be to finance and organize a municipal formation movement. The literature on business location decisions points to the fact that the taxes businesses attend to in these location decisions are almost exclusively state taxes.[1] Other aspects of the local business climate are considered more important than local taxes; in particular, businesses are interested in labor availability and unionization and links to transportation networks. When businesses are concerned about taxes in their location decisions, the taxes are state ones. The argument here is that businesses will not pay great attention to local taxes unless state taxes are already congenial enough for the business to want to stay in the state. Where state taxes are congenial to businesses, businesses have incentives to remain in the state and to work to lower their local taxes. Where state taxes are onerous, *businesses concerned with taxes* have an incentive simply to leave the state. Evidence from studies of business location decisions suggests that one class of businesspersons—manufacturers—is particularly sensitive to taxes. These businesspersons should be the most willing to underwrite the creation of cities to lower their taxes.[2]

The analyses employ three measures to indicate incentives for entrepreneurial involvement in municipal formation: (1) whether there is a manufacturer in the county, (2) the rate of state corporate income taxation for corporate incomes of $25,000 or more, and (3) whether there are state-imposed taxation limits for municipalities that would decrease the incentives for manufacturers to form new municipalities. The first measure—whether there is a manufacturer in the county—is transparent. There have to be manufacturers in the county for them to serve as entrepreneurs. The second measure requires more justification. Where state corporate taxes are *low*, businesses have a *greater* incentive to lead a movement for the formation of a new local government. The business is already located in a congenial state and has little *tax* reason to move elsewhere. Thus the business—largely tax-sensitive manufacturing firms—would have more incentive to invest in altering local tax structures. Where state corporate taxes are high, concern about taxes should push the business to move to a more congenial state and *not* to form a new local government that simply cannot affect *state* taxation levels. For the third measure, where taxes are already limited, manufacturers do not have to be as concerned about social service burdens leading to higher taxes because the state has taken care of that inconvenience. The particular tax limit I use is the tax levy limit, which specifies "a maximum allowed percentage increase from the prior year" or "a maximum percentage of income that tax revenue can take."[3] This variable is coded 1 when the state places a tax levy limit on either municipalities or counties; otherwise, it takes a value of 0.

The measures for solutions to the collective action problem of special district formation are the number of real estate developers in the county at the beginning of the decade, the two annexation law measures, and median family income for special districts; and, for municipalities, whether there is a manufacturing establishment at the beginning of the decade, the rate of state corporate taxation at the beginning of the decade, and whether there is a state-imposed tax levy limit upon municipalities and counties. There is one exception to this picture. For the 1950s, there are no data on the number of real estate developers in counties at the beginning of the decade, so I use the number of real estate and financial firms instead. I take the log of this number because I expect the effect of a one-unit change in the number of real estate and financial concerns to begin to tail off as the number of firms becomes quite large. This is the least-aggregated measure available for the 1950s.

There are several measures for service pressures. First, population pressure is essentially pressure for new services. The reason more governments might form where there is a larger population is simply that more people need more services, and more complicated services, than do fewer people. Population pressure is included here, measured by the log of the population at the beginning of the decade and by the percentage change in population in the previous decade. I use the log of the population because the effect of an increase in population should become smaller as the population becomes larger. Second, for municipalities, increasing income is another indicator of the need for new services. I thus include median family income at the beginning of the decade for municipalities. Third, for special districts alone, tax levy limits indicate the inability of existing local governments to provide new services; the effect of these limits should be to encourage the formation of new special districts.[4]

I measure taxation worries leading to the formation of cities by how difficult it is for municipalities to annex. Taxation is the one reason for municipal formation where entrepreneurs and citizens have the same motivation. As noted in the cases in Chapter 2, when citizens feared annexation, the operative part of this fear was concern about higher taxes. Consequently, when annexation requirements are important in the formation of municipalities in a particular decade, I interpret this as evidence of tax limitation reasons acting effectively in the formation of cities. Citizens wish to incorporate defensively in order to ensure lower taxes than exist in the city wishing to annex them. Annexation requirements differ across states: In some states, annexation is illegal; in others, annexation is unilateral, without the opportunity for objection on the part of the to-be-annexed citizens; and in still others, annexation is legal, but the to-be-annexed citizens have a means to resist. I measure these differences with two variables. The first is whether the state allows unilateral annexation. The second is whether the state allows annexation, but the citizens to be annexed have an effective voice in the annexation process; if they must initiate the annexation process or if a referendum on annexation must succeed among them, then this variable is coded 1. The remaining states, those that do not allow annexation, fall into the intercept of the equations and provide the standard of comparison for the effects of these variables. Thus, for municipalities, we should expect the coefficients on these two variables to be positive in the 1960s, 1970s, and 1980s, given the increased incentives for forming cities as walls against higher taxes in those decades. Citizens in counties where annexation is legal should incorporate more municipalities than citizens in counties where annexation is illegal.

I measure race and ethnicity by the number of nonwhite, African-American, or Latino residents in a county at the beginning of the decade. The censuses for the 1950s and 1960s reported statistics only in terms of white/nonwhite. The census for the 1980s was the first to report the number of Latino residents in the county. There is nothing magic about this particular measure; others, such as change in the number or percentage of African-American residents, and work equally well. We should expect effects for municipalities in the 1950s and 1960s (and perhaps in the 1980s). To anticipate the results in Chapter 5, I also assessed the effects of the presence of poor populations upon municipal formation to ensure that the racial effects documented in Chapter 5 are not simply income effects in disguise. They are not.

There are supply limits upon this process of governmental formation. By "supply," I mean state and federal laws that affect the difficulty of forming municipalities or special districts. Where it is more difficult to form a city, the supply of cities is lower. The factors discussed to this point constitute the *demand* for new local governments; the difficulty of forming a new government affects the extent to which the demand leads to the creation of a new government. I measure these constraints by (1) whether municipalities can be created only through a special act of the legislature at the beginning of the decade, (2) the number of special district enabling laws in the state at the beginning of the decade, and (3) whether Section 5 of the Voting Rights Act covers the county in the decade in question.[5] Where the formation of municipalities requires a special act of the legislature, the supply of municipalities is restricted; we should expect there to be fewer municipal formations (and perhaps more special district formations). Where there are more general enabling laws for special districts, the supply is greater; we should expect more special districts to form. As citizens become more and more concerned about local taxes and less interested in forming service cities, more special district general enabling laws should encourage the formation of more municipalities; access to special districts makes these new cities less expensive. Where the Voting Rights Act preclearance requirements are in effect, the supply of all types of local governments is lower; thus we should expect fewer special districts and, perhaps, fewer municipal formations.

The Voting Rights Act, however, should also affect demand; it should affect the ability of whites desiring racial exclusion to ensure an all-white politics. Because the Voting Rights Act has these two potential effects, the coefficient estimates for this variable indicate the *net* effect of the Voting Rights Act: the influence on demand minus the influence on supply. When the coefficient is insignificant, the Voting Rights Act either affects supply and demand equally or has no effect. Where the coefficient is positive, the effect on the demand outweighs the effect on supply. Where the coefficient is negative, the effect on supply outweighs the effect on demand.

The argument is that entrepreneurs and small groups enable collective actions to succeed; thus, by and large, I include interactions between conditions for emergence of a political entrepreneur or small group and the collective pressures. The exceptions to this pattern occur when, after extensive testing, it was clear that the particular variable was powerful in its own right and that the interaction with entrepreneurial conditions or with the presence of developers was statistically insignificant. In performing this test, I included the variables alone and with their interactions with entrepreneurial conditions; this was done to ensure that I tested my model of entrepreneurial and small-group influence rather than simply assuming it.

The values of the variables change over time. Annexation laws, for example, are not the same in 1960 as they are twenty years later; assuming that they are the same would introduce a severe distortion into the analyses. Special district enabling laws are enacted and abolished over the thirty-five-year period. Section 5 of the Voting Rights Act extends to more and more counties over the thirty-seven years. And so on. I note the year in which the value of the variable was recorded for the particular analyses in Appendix C.[6]

The Model

One obvious question is why I did not weight the sample by population. The main reason for not weighting is that I want to generalize to counties in the United States—without an urban bias in the analysis. The question the analyses address is why governments form in the United States, not why they form in population centers in the United States. Moreover, I want to evaluate, not assume, the hypothesis that larger populations lead to the formation of more governments. Thus, the sample is unweighted. The model specifications control for a number of factors—population, for example—that make counties different from one another.

The results reported in Chapter 5 are from Poisson regressions. These are more appropriate than linear-Normal regressions because the dependent variable is a discrete, rare event, and there are probably more 0s and 1s than other observations and the distribution probably tails off from there. It makes little sense, then, to assume that the number of government formations is distributed Normally—that it is a continuous variable ranging from almost negative infinity to almost positive infinity. The assumption I make is more plausible. There (logically) cannot be a negative number of formations; the functional form of the systematic component is specified to bound the predicted values at zero.[7] The systematic component, then, has an exponential form, and the stochastic component is Poisson.[8] Throughout, I employ robust standard errors to ensure that inferences based upon the estimation results are robust to deviations from the Poisson model.

Because the systematic component is exponential instead of linear, the coefficient estimates must be inserted back into the exponential form in order to interpret them. With a linear-Normal (ordinary least squares) estimation, the systematic component is simply $X\beta$. For every one-unit increase in X, there is a β-unit increase in the dependent variable. The systematic component here is $e^{X\beta}$. To calculate the effect of a change in x upon y, we have to evaluate $e^{X\beta}$ for the new value of x, and then again for the old value of x, and then subtract; the result is the effect upon the dependent variable of this particular change in the explanatory variable. I calculate the effects of the variables throughout the presentation in order to place the estimation results in terms of real politics.

APPENDIX C

Coefficient Estimates
and Robust Standard Errors

Comparison of the Coefficient Estimates

Tables C.1 and C.2 present all of the coefficient estimates, along with their robust standard errors. I present simply a comparison of the coefficient estimates over time. The goal of this comparison is to bolster the argument that the coefficient estimates presented in Chapter 5 constitute a stable picture of the politics of local government formation over this thirty-seven-year period. Inspecting these two tables leads to the conclusion that even though the analyses cover thirty-seven years of politics, when variables appear in the equations, their coefficient estimates are of the same sign and magnitude as in the other equations where they appear. *None* of the coefficient estimates change magnitude or sign. In fact, the stability of the coefficient estimates is remarkable.

Table C.1. Municipality Coefficient Estimates

Variable	1950s	1960s	1970s	1980s
Population change, preceding decade	0.01			
Log of population	0.33	0.55		
Number of Latino residents				0.05
Entrepreneur interacted with Latino residents				−0.004

132

Table C.1. (*Continued*)

Number of nonwhite residents	−0.13	−0.08		
Entrepreneur interacted with nonwhite residents	0.02	0.01		
Entrepreneur interacted with median income	0.00003			
Unilateral annexation		10.12	7.64	
Annexation with defense		10.16	8.24	9.86
Tax levy limit	−8.69		−8.57	
Tax interacted with manufacturers			0.04	
Manufacturers	8.97	8.34	7.70	9.32
Special act of incorporation	−9.04			−10.98
Special district enabling laws		0.04	0.05	
Voting Rights Act				1.60
Intercept	−12.46	−22.10	−19.48	−22.55

Table C.2. Special District Coefficient Estimates

Variable	1950s	1960s	1970s	1980s
Population change, preceding decade	0.006			
Log of population	0.47	0.44	0.18	
Number of Latino residents residents				0.01
Number of nonwhite residents	−0.15			
Entrepreneur interacted with nonwhite residents	0.02			
Entrepreneur interacted with median income		−0.00009		
Number of developers		0.43		
Tax levy limit	0.83		0.54	
Special district enabling laws	0.06	0.05	0.08	0.12
Voting Rights Act		−1.08	−0.68	−1.24
Unilateral annexation			−1.22	−1.51
Annexation with defense			−1.18	−0.96
Intercept	−2.22	−1.74	−0.25	−1.74

Tables Presenting the Coefficients and Robust Standard Errors for the Preceding Analyses

Table C.3. Special District Formations in the 1950s, Poisson Regression

Variable	Coefficient Estimate	Robust Standard Error
Population change, 1940–50	0.006	0.003
Log of the population 1950	0.47	0.10
Number of nonwhite residents, 1950	−0.15	0.06
Interaction between number of nonwhite residents and the log of the number of financial and real estate concerns, 1950	0.02	0.008
Tax levy limit, 1970	0.83	0.27
Number of special district enabling laws, 1952	0.06	0.01
Intercept	−2.22	0.37
N: 198 Log-likelihood: −114.05		

Table C.4. Municipal Formations in the 1950s, Poisson Regression

Variable	Coefficient Estimate	Robust Standard Error
Population change, 1940–50	0.01	0.004
Log of population, 1950	0.33	0.19
Number of nonwhite residents, 1950	−0.13	0.03
Corporate tax 1950, interacted with number of nonwhite residents	0.02	0.005
Corporate tax 1950, interacted with median family income, 1950	0.00003	0.00003
Tax levy limit, 1970	−8.69	0.78
Whether there are two manufacturers in the county, 1950	8.97	0.70
Whether a special act is required to incorporate, 1952	−9.04	0.40
Intercept	−12.46	0.84
N: 194 Log-likelihood: −59.06		

Table C.5. Special District Formations in the 1960s, Poisson Regression

Variable	Robust Coefficient Estimate	Standard Error
Log of population, 1960	0.44	0.06
Number of developers, 1960, interacted with median family income, 1960	−0.00009	0.00002
Number of developers, 1960	0.43	0.10
Number of special district enabling laws, 1962	0.05	0.01
Voting Rights Act coverage, 1965	−1.08	0.30
Intercept	−1.74	0.22
N: 197		
Log-likelihood: −126.6		

Table C.6. Municipal Formations in the 1960s, Poisson Regression

Variable	Coefficient Estimate	Robust Standard Error
Log of population, 1960	0.55	0.11
Number of nonwhite residents, 1960	−0.08	0.009
Corporate taxes, 1960, interacted with the number of nonwhite residents, 1960	0.01	0.001
Whether there is a manufacturer, 1960	8.34	0.60
Number of special district enabling laws, 1962	0.04	0.02
Annexation allowed; citizens of area to be annexed have *no* channel of recourse, 1960	10.12	0.70
Annexation allowed; citizens of area to be annexed have at least one channel of recourse, 1960	10.16	0.48
Intercept	−22.10	0.70
N: 199		
Log-likelihood: −87.98		

Table C.7.   Special District Formations in the 1970s, Poisson Regression

Variable	Coefficient Estimate	Robust Standard Error
Log of population, 1970	0.18	0.05
Tax levy limit, 1970	0.54	0.46
Number of special district enabling laws, 1972	0.08	0.02
Voting Rights Act coverage, 1975	−0.68	0.36
Annexation allowed; citizens to be annexed have *no* channel of recourse, 1978	−1.22	0.39
Annexation allowed; citizens to be annexed have at least one channel of recourse, 1978	−1.18	0.32
Intercept	−0.25	0.28

N: 198
Log-likelihood: −130.62

Table C.8.   Municipal Formations in the 1970s, Poisson Regression

Variable	Coefficient Estimate	Robust Standard Error
Corporate taxes, 1970, interacted with the log of the number of manufacturers, 1970	0.04	0.01
Tax levy limit, 1970	−8.57	0.68
Whether there is a manufacturer in the county, 1970	7.70	0.66
Number of special district enabling laws, 1972	0.05	0.03
Annexation allowed; citizens to be annexed have *no* channel of recourse, 1978	7.64	0.78
Annexation allowed; citizens to be annexed have at least one channel of recourse, 1978	8.24	0.46
Intercept	−19.48	0.63

N: 199
Log-likelihood: −69.43

Table C.9. Special District Formations in the 1980s, Poisson Regression

Variable	Coefficient Estimate	Robust Standard Error
Number of Latino residents, 1980	0.01	0.002
Number of special district enabling laws, 1982	0.12	0.03
Voting Rights Act coverage, 1980	−1.24	0.57
Annexation allowed; citizens to be annexed have *no* channel of recourse, 1978	−1.51	0.69
Annexation allowed; citizens to be annexed have at least one channel of recourse, 1978	−0.96	0.54
Intercept	−1.74	0.55

N: 200
Log-likelihood: −113.28

Table C.10. Municipal Formations in the 1980s, Poisson Regression

Variable	Coefficient Estimate	Robust Standard Errors
Number of Latino residents, 1980	0.05	0.009
Corporate taxes, 1980, interacted with the number of Latino residents, 1980	−0.004	0.001
Whether there is a manufacturer, 1980	9.32	0.66
Whether incorporation requires a special act of the legislature, 1982	−10.98	0.44
Voting Rights Act coverage, 1980	1.60	0.61
Annexation legal; citizens to be annexed have at least one channel of recourse, 1978	9.86	0.39
Intercept	−22.55	0.59

N: 200
Log-likelihood: −33.92

Table C.11. Municipal Formations in the 1950s with Consideration of Poor Populations, Poisson Regression

Variable	Coefficient Estimate	Robust Standard Error
Population change, 1940–50	0.01	0.004
Log of population, 1950	0.36	0.24
Number of nonwhite residents, 1950	−0.25	0.06
Corporate tax, 1950, interacted with number of nonwhite residents	0.04	0.01
Corporate tax, 1950, interacted with median family income, 1950	0.00007	0.00004
Tax levy limit, 1970	−8.54	0.84
Whether there are two manufacturers in the county, 1950	9.08	0.68
Whether a special act is required to incorporate, 1952	−8.80	0.43
Number of families with incomes under $2,000, 1949	0.35	0.15
Corporate tax, 1950, interacted with number of families with incomes under $2,000	−0.06	0.03
Intercept	−13.32	1.11

N: 194
Log-likelihood: −56.67

Table C.12. Municipal Formations in the 1960s with Consideration of Poor Families, Poisson Regression

Variable	Coefficient Estimate	Robust Standard Error
Log of population, 1960	0.77	0.20
Number of nonwhite residents, 1960	−0.20	0.06
Corporate taxes, 1960, interacted with the number of nonwhite residents, 1960	0.03	0.009
Whether there is a manufacturer, 1960	7.81	0.72
Number of special district enabling laws, 1962	0.04	0.02
Annexation allowed; citizens of area to be annexed have *no* channel of recourse, 1960	10.02	0.70
Annexation allowed; citizens of area to be annexed have at one channel of recourse, 1960	9.89	0.47
Number of families with incomes under $3,000, 1959	0.14	0.09
Corporate tax, 1960, interacted with number of families with incomes under $3,000	−0.03	0.02
Intercept	−21.78	0.79

N: 197
Log-likelihood: −87.06

APPENDIX D

Sample Counties

1. Wade Hampton, AK
2. Jefferson, AL
3. Lee, AL
4. Macon, AL
5. Marion, AL
6. Winston, AL
7. Baxter, AR
8. Crawford, AR
9. Dallas, AR
10. Stone, AR
11. Coconino, AZ
12. Santa Cruz, AZ
13. Amador, CA
14. Contra Costa, CA
15. San Luis Obispo, CA
16. Santa Cruz, CA
17. Shasta, CA
18. Sutter, CA
19. Trinity, CA
20. Ventura, CA
21. Bent, CO
22. Phillips, CO
23. New Haven, CT
24. Broward, FL
25. Hernando, FL
26. Baldwin, GA
27. Banks, GA
28. Coffee, GA
29. Dawson, GA
30. Glascock, GA
31. Hall, GA
32. Jasper, GA
33. Long, GA
34. Mitchell, GA
35. Morgan, GA
36. Whitfield, GA
37. Cedar, IA
38. Howard, IA
39. Jones, IA
40. Madison, IA
41. Marshall, IA
42. Sac, IA
43. Winnebago, IA
44. Caribou, ID
45. Lemhi, ID
46. Payette, ID
47. Stephenson, IL
48. Dearborn, IN

49. Jay, IN
50. Porter, IN
51. Lyon, KS
52. Saline, KS
53. Henry, KY
54. Claiborne, LA
55. Concordia, LA
56. Morehouse, LA
57. St. Charles, LA
58. Barnstable, MA
59. Berkshire, MA
60. Baltimore City, MD
61. Knox, ME
62. Somerset, ME
63. York, ME
64. Arenac, MI
65. Branch, MI
66. Macomb, MI
67. Marquette, MI
68. Muskegon, MI
69. Ontonagon, MI
70. Wexford, MI
71. Chisago, MN
72. Clay, MN
73. Cook, MN
74. Meeker, MN
75. Pennington, MN
76. Swift, MN
77. Andrew, MO
78. Carroll, MO
79. Cedar, MO
80. Oregon, MO
81. Osage, MO
82. Alcorn, MS
83. Itawamba, MS
84. Jasper, MS
85. Lee, MS
86. Warren, MS
87. Wilkinson, MS
88. Golden Valley, MT
89. Pondera, MT
90. Silver Bow, MT
91. Ashe, NC
92. Avery, NC
93. Carteret, NC
94. Caswell, NC
95. Chatham, NC
96. Gates, NC
97. Guilford, NC
98. Perquimans, NC
99. Wake, NC
100. Washington, NC
101. Yancey, NC
102. Billings, ND
103. Burke, ND
104. Pembina, ND
105. Richland, ND
106. Williams, ND
107. Cass, NE
108. Cedar, NE
109. Clay, NE
110. Dixon, NE
111. Dodge, NE
112. Holt, NE
113. Logan, NE
114. Phelps, NE
115. Sullivan, NH
116. Middlesex, NJ
117. Passaic, NJ
118. Dona Ana, NM
119. Grant, NM
120. Lea, NM
121. Socorro, NM
122. Esmeralda, NV
123. Lincoln, NV
124. Monroe, NY
125. Morgan, OH
126. Morrow, OH

127. Perry, OH
128. Ross, OH
129. Shelby, OH
130. Wood, OH
131. Cimarron, OK
132. Kiowa, OK
133. Le Flore, OK
134. Muskogee, OK
135. Umatilla, OR
136. Blair, PA
137. Clarion, PA
138. Huntingdon, PA
139. Juniata, PA
140. Lebanon, PA
141. Northumberland, PA
142. Perry, PA
143. Westmoreland, PA
144. Newport, RI
145. Aurora, SD
146. Brown, SD
147. Faulk, SD
148. Kingsbury, SD
149. Miner, SD
150. Potter, SD
151. Tripp, SD
152. Turner, SD
153. Franklin, TN
154. Hardeman, TN
155. Humphreys, TN
156. Lincoln, TN
157. Wayne, TN
158. Bailey, TX
159. Dallam, TX
160. Donley, TX
161. Duval, TX
162. El Paso, TX
163. Fayette, TX

164. Harrison, TX
165. Lavaca, TX
166. Liberty, TX
167. Limestone, TX
168. Live Oak, TX
169. Marion, TX
170. Milam, TX
171. Mitchell, TX
172. Starr, TX
173. Stephens, TX
174. Willacy, TX
175. Davis, UT
176. Weber, UT
177. Bland, VA
178. Charlotte, VA
179. Chesterfield, VA
180. Essex, VA
181. Franklin, VA
182. Middlesex, VA
183. Northumberland, VA
184. Sussex, VA
185. Douglas, WA
186. Grant, WA
187. Mason, WA
188. Ashland, WI
189. Crawford, WI
190. Door, WI
191. Forest, WI
192. Juneau, WI
193. Boone, WV
194. Braxton, WV
195. Fayette, WV
196. Randolph, WV
197. Roane, WV
198. Summers, WV
199. Webster, WV
200. Campbell, WY

NOTES

Chapter 1

1. Yorty's testimony before the U.S. Senate Subcommittee on Executive Reorganization as quoted in Roland Liebert, *Disintegration and Political Action* (New York: Academic Press, 1976), p. 9.

2. The fact that suburbanization around London at the turn of the twentieth century resulted in the creation of no new cities is suggestive of the oddity of American behavior. Even though new communities did not coincide with existing local governments, these English suburbanites felt no need for their own political structures. See Alan A. Jackson, *Semi-Detached London: Suburban Development, Life and Transport, 1900–39* (London: George Allen & Unwin, Ltd., 1973); Eric H. Monkkonen, *America Becomes Urban: The Development of U.S. Cities and Towns 1780–1980* (Berkeley: University of California Press, 1988), pp. 69, 74–5.

3. Donald Foster Stetzer, *Special Districts in Cook County* (Chicago: University of Chicago Department of Geography, Research Paper No. 169, 1975), p. 52.

A resident of Western Springs, a Chicago suburb, would be governed by eight districts: the Forest Preserve District of Cook County, the Suburban TB Sanitarium District, the Metropolitan Sanitary District of Greater Chicago, the Des Plains Valley Mosquito Abatement District, the Western Springs Park District, the Lyons Mental Health District, the West Suburban Mass Transit District, and the Hospital Governing Commission. See Bryan D. Jones, *Government Urban America* (Boston: Little, Brown, 1983), p. 203

4. Throughout this chapter, I present statistics derived from my analyses of the data from the 1987 Census of Governments data tape and from my coding of the state laws regarding special districts and municipalities that are catalogued in the U.S. Bureau of the Census, Census of Governments, *Government Organization* volumes from 1952 through 1987. Unless otherwise noted, these were my sources of information.

5. See the advice in Michael Sumichrist and Ronald G. Shafer, *The New Complete Book of Home Buying* (New York: Bantam, 1988); Michael C. Murphy, *How to Buy a Home While You Can Still Afford To*, rev. ed, (New York: Sterling, 1989).

6. I rely heavily here on the understanding of institutions and organizations

developed in Douglass North, *Institutions, Institutional Change and Economic Performance* (Cambridge: Cambridge University Press, 1990).

7. See the evidence in Gary Miller, *Cities by Contract* (Cambridge: MIT Press, 1981); Michael N. Danielson, *The Politics of Exclusion* (New York: Columbia University Press, 1976); Gregory Weiher, "Public Policy and Patterns of Residential Segregation," *Western Political Quarterly* 42 (December 1989):651–77; Gregory R. Weiher, *The Fractured Metropolis* (Albany: State University of New York Press, 1991); John R. Logan and Mark Schneider, "Racial Segregation and Racial Change in American Suburbs, 1970–1980," *American Journal of Sociology* 89(n.4 1984):874–88; John R. Logan and Mark Schneider, "The Stratification of Metropolitan Suburbs, 1960–1970," *American Sociological Review* 46(n.2 1981):175–86; Harry J. Holzer, "The Spatial Mismatch Hypothesis: What Has the Evidence Shown?" *Urban Studies* 28 (February, 1991):105–22.

The zoning powers of new cities have also been employed to zone out certain religious practices and thus people of certain religions. See William Glaberson, "Orthodox Jews Battle Neighbors in a Zoning War," *New York Times*, June 3, 1991, pp. A1, B12.

8. Robert M. Stein, *Urban Alternatives: Public and Private Markets in the Provision of Local Services* (Pittsburgh: University of Pittsburgh Press, 1990), p. 33. Interestingly, Stein finds no difference between older and younger cities (among the 317 cities he examines) in per capita spending on housing, federal welfare, local welfare, fire protection, or highways.

9. Robert G. Smith, *Ad Hoc Governments* (Beverly Hills: Sage, 1974), p. 59; *Sayler Land Co. v. Tulare Lake Basin Water Storage District*, 410 U.S. 719 (1973); *Ball v. James*, 451 U.S. 355 (1981); Joan C. Williams, "The Constitutional Vulnerability of American Local Government: The Politics of City Status in American Law," *Wisconsin Law Review* (1986):83; Gerald E. Frug, *Local Government Law* (St. Paul: West, 1988), pp. 606–16.

10. John C. Bollens, *Special District Governments in the United States* (Berkeley: University of California Press, 1957), p. 146.

11. In Arizona, for example,

> to sign an antinoxious weed district formation petition, one need only be a district landowner. But to vote for district formation or for a board member one must also be a district resident. This combination is almost reversed in the case of the hospital district, in which to be a petitioner one need be only a state elector within the area of the proposed district. To vote on district formation or the board of directors, however, one must also be a district real property owner. Sanitary districts add another dimension to petition-voter complexity, depending on the means of formation. Such districts may be established by action of the supervisors if petitioned by a majority of landowners or by owners of a majority of land in the proposed district. Alternately, a district may be formed by an election if petition is by at least 25 taxpayers.

See Don L. Bowen, "Reshaping Special District Government in Arizona," *Arizona Review* 32(Winter, n.1, 1984):18.

12. Virginia Marion Perrenod, *Special Districts, Special Purposes* (College Station: Texas A & M University Press, 1984), p. 47, emphasis added.

13. Bowen, "Reshaping Special District Government in Arizona," p. 20.

14. Douglas Arthur Stark, "Patterns of Legislator Incumbency in Independent Taxing Non-School Special Districts of California" (unpublished Ph.D. dissertation, University of Southern California, 1971), p. 102.

15. Bowen, "Reshaping Special District Government in Arizona," p. 16.

16. Douglas R. Porter, "Financing Infrastructure with Special Districts," *Urban Land* 46(May, n.5, 1987):13.

17. "Citizens Deserve Facts, Input," *The Centre Daily Times*, State College, Pennsylvania, August 10, 1989, p. A-10.

18. Stark, "Patterns of Legislator Incumbency in Independent Taxing Non-School Special Districts of California," p. 100.

19. Bollens, *Special District Governments in the United States*, p. 37.

20. Albert K. Karnig and B. Oliver Walter, "Decline in Municipal Voter Turnout," *American Politics Quarterly* 11(4, October 1983):496.

21. Ann O'M. Bowman and Richard C. Kearney, *State and Local Government*, 2nd ed. (Boston: Houghton Mifflin, 1993), p. 119; Edward C. Banfield and James Q. Wilson, *City Politics* (New York: Vintage, 1963), p. 225. Of course, participation does not consist only of voting, and accountability is not simply a function of voter turnout. There are differences among cities in the amount of other forms of participation (such as contacting municipal officials) and in the responsiveness of local officials to political participation. For evidence on this point, see Sidney Verba and Norman H. Nie, *Participation in America* (New York: Harper and Row, 1972), chapters 2 and 13 and part III.

22. In 1957, property taxes and intergovernmental transfers composed only one-quarter of the revenue of special districts. Service charges, special assessments, rates, and rents composed the remainder (Bollens, *Special District Governments in the United States*, p. 41).
As can be seen from Tables 1.4 and 1.5, special districts have been beneficiaries of federal aid. This funding occurred initially in the natural resources area as federal monies were made available to soil conservation, drainage, flood control, and irrigation districts. More recently, federal government influence has been present in the establishment of housing and urban renewal agencies and districts involved with airports, sewage disposal, and other environmental controls. Special districts were a major beneficiary of federal aid policies in the 1970s. See Scott A. Bollens, "Examining the Link Between State Policy and the Creation of Local Special Districts," *State and Local Government Review* (Fall 1986):119. In 1981–82 the major targets of federal aid were districts concerned with housing and community development and sewerage.

23. Bowen, "Reshaping Special District Government in Arizona," p. 20.

24. Bollens, *Special District Governments in the United States*, p. 44; U.S. Department of Commerce, *Census of Governments* (Washington, DC: U.S. Government Printing Office, 1987), v. 1.

25. Henry A. Coleman, "Government by Special Districts" (unpublished Ph.D. dissertation, Princeton University, 1979), p. 40.

26. Of the long-term debt, $10 billion was for housing and community development, $6 billion for sewerage, $12 billion for water supply, $46 billion for electric power, $5 billion for transit, and $200 million for gas.

27. Alberta Sbragia, "Cities, Capital, and Banks," in Kenneth Newton, ed., *Urban Political Economy* (New York: St. Martin's Press, 1981), p. 203.

28. Sbragia, "Cities, Capital, and Banks," p. 208. This source of funding is not inconsequential. Because special districts have the ability to use revenue bonds and because municipalities generally rely upon general obligation bonds, when the federal government reduces its financial commitment to municipalities, there is an important incentive for local governments, businesses, and developers to turn to special districts as a way to continue to provide or receive services.

29. Ronald C. Fisher, *State and Local Public Finance* (Glenview, IL: Scott, Foresman, 1988), p. 345.

30. Fisher, *State and Local Public Finance*, pp. 120, 166.

31. Fisher, *State and Local Public Finance*, p. 214. Municipal governments vary significantly in their tax rates. See Helen F. Ladd and Katharine L. Bradbury, "City Taxes and Property Tax Bases," *National Tax Journal* 41(December 1988):503–23. Older cities, perhaps not surprisingly, tend to have the highest taxes of all. See Robert M. Stein, *Urban Alternatives: Public and Private Markets in the Provision of Local Services* (Pittsburgh: University of Pittsburgh Press, 1990), p. 33. Municipal governments are more often subject to state-imposed tax, expenditure, and debt limits than are special districts. See David Merriman, *The Control of Municipal Budgets* (New York: Quorum Books, 1987). See the articles in Helen F. Ladd and T. Nicolaus Tideman, *Tax and Expenditure Limitations* (Washington, DC: The Urban Institute, 1981).

32. Neil D. McFeeley, "Special District Governments: The New Dark Continent Twenty Years Later," *Midwest Review of Public Administration* 2(December, n.4, 1978):211–45; Bollens, "Examining the Link Between State Policy and the Creation of Local Special Districts."

33. Bollens, *Special District Governments in the United States*, pp. 6–15.

34. McFeeley, "Special District Governments"; Robert L. Morlan, "Local Governments: An Embarrassment of Riches," in James W. Fesler, ed., *The 50 States and Their Local Governments* (New York: Alfred A. Knopf, 1967), pp. 505–49; Stetzer, *Special Districts in Cook County*.

35. S. J. Makielski, Jr., and David G. Temple, *Special District Government in Virginia* (Charlottesville: University of Virginia, Institute of Government, 1967), p. 78; Merriman, *The Control of Municipal Budgets*, p. 23; Terry Nichols Clark and Lorna Crowley Ferguson, *City Money* (New York: Columbia University Press, 1983), p. 239; Stetzer, *Special Districts in Cook County*, p. 48; J. Richard Aronson and John L. Hilley, *Financing State and Local Governments*, 4th ed. (Washington, DC: Brookings Institution, 1986), pp. 76–7; Coleman, "Government by Special Districts," pp. 8–9; Clarence N. Stone, Robert K. Whelan, and William J. Murin, *Urban Policy and Politics in a Bureaucratic Age*, 2nd ed. (Englewood Cliffs, NJ: Prentice-Hall, 1986), p. 46; David L. Chicoine and Norman Walzer, *Governmental Structure and Local Public Finance* (Boston: Oelgeschlager, Gunn, & Hain, 1985), pp. 71–4.

The exceptions to this explanation come from public choice scholars who have argued recently that "The difficulty citizens have in indicating preferences is one reason most areas have several overlapping local units of government providing different services." See Vincent Ostrom, Robert Bish, and Elinor Ostrom, *Local Government in the United States* (San Francisco: Institute for Contemporary Studies, 1988), p. 93.

36. Robert C. Wood, *1400 Governments* (Cambridge: Harvard University Press, 1961), p. 30; Platon N. Rigos and Charles J. Spindler, "Municipal Incorporation Activity: Why New Cities Are Created," paper prepared for delivery at the Annual Conference of the American Political Science Association, Atlanta, Georgia, September 3, 1989.

37. Gary L. Miller, *Cities by Contract: The Politics of Municipal Incorporation* (Cambridge: MIT Press, 1981).

38. Michael W. Danielson, *The Politics of Exclusion* (New York: Columbia University Press, 1976).

39. Miller, *Cities by Contract*, p. 36; Jon C. Teaford, *City and Suburb: The Political Fragmentation of Metropolitan America, 1650–1970* (Baltimore: Johns Hopkins University Press, 1979), p. 24.

40. Miller, *Cities by Contract*, and Teaford, *City and Suburb*, are notable exceptions to this pattern.

41. Mancur Olson, *The Logic of Collective Action* (Cambridge: Harvard University Press, 1965); Peter Ordeshook, *Game Theory and Political Theory* (Cambridge: Cambridge University Press, 1986), pp. 210–11, 222–224.

42. Olson, *The Logic of Collective Action*.

43. Note that one common solution to collective action problems—selective incentives—is not part of this set, although in the discussion to come there are instances of the use of selective incentives. These selective incentive solutions are just much rarer than the other solutions, given the nature of the collective action problem.

44. Olson, *The Logic of Collective Action*.

45. Terry Moe, *The Organization of Interests* (Chicago: University of Chicago Press, 1980).

46. Doug McAdam, *Political Process and the Development of Black Insurgency, 1930–1970* (Chicago: University of Chicago Press, 1982).

47. Louis Uchitelle, "States and Cities Are Pushing Hard for Higher Taxes," *New York Times*, March 25, 1991, pp. A1, C6.

48. Robert Waste, "The Early Years in the Life Cycle of City Councils," *Urban Studies* 20(1983):73–81.

Chapter 2

1. The citizens of Levittown, Pennsylvania, continue to try to incorporate; their latest effort was in 1989. They have thus far failed (personal communication with Alan Levine, Department of Government, Harvard University, Cambridge, MA). The quotation is from Incorporation Study Committee of the Levittown Civic Association, "A Study of the Factors Involved in the Incorporation of Levittown, Bucks County, PA" (Levittown, PA: Levittown Civic Association, 1954).

2. Included in Appendix B of Reynaldo F. Macias, Guillermo Vicente Flores, Donaldo Figueroa, and Luis Aragon, *A Study of Unincorporated East Los Angeles*, Monograph No. 3 (Los Angeles: UCLA, Chicano Studies Center, 1973). East Los Angeles, too, has a string of incorporation attempts with no successes.

3. Howard Lee McBain, *The Law and the Practice of Municipal Home Rule* (New York: Columbia University Press, 1916), p. 59

4. McBain, *The Law and the Practice of Municipal Home Rule*, p. 59.

5. Robin L. Einhorn, *Property Rules: Political Economy in Chicago, 1833–1872* (Chicago: University of Chicago Press, 1991).

6. Mark I. Gelfand, *A Nation of Cities: The Federal Government and Urban America, 1933–1965* (New York: Oxford University Press, 1975), p. 114. Nelson wrote in 1949 to the president of NAREB:

> I do not believe in democracy. I think it stinks. I believe in a republic operated by elected representatives who are permitted to do the job, as the board of directors should. I don't think anybody except direct taxpayers should be allowed to vote.

As Gelfand notes, "Not surprisingly, proposals carrying the NAREB imprint were more likely to enhance property rather than human values." See Gelfand, *A Nation of Cities*, p. 113.

7. Moreover, according to Friedland, "Interviews with developers indicated that powers of eminent domain were the most important feature of urban renewal. Since vacant space was decreasingly available and central city land ownership

highly fragmented, the assembly of a large parcel remained cumbersome and costly, as small owners held out for high prices or refused to sell altogether." See Roger Friedland, *Power and Crisis in the City* (London: Macmillan, 1983), p. 82.

8. "Plan Drafted for Re-development of East Detroit," *The Michigan Daily*, Ann Arbor, MI, October 1, 1990, v. CI, n. 18, pp. 1–2; Angie Cannon, "'A New Town Within a City' for Detroiters," *Detroit Free Press and News*, September 30, 1990, pp. 1A, 8A.

9. "Plan Drafted for Re-development of East Detroit," pp. 1–2; personal communication with Jonathan Simon, University of Michigan Department of Political Science, Ann Arbor, Michigan.

10. Douglas R. Porter, Ben C. Lin, and Richard B. Peiser, *Special Districts: A Useful Technique for Financing Infrastructure* (Washington, D.C.: Urban Land Institute, 1987). They say:

> Although developers apply to the commission for permission to create a MUD, majority vote of the new district's residents is required. . . . Once the application is approved, the developer sells tax-exempt revenue bonds through local underwriters. The bonds are backed by the taxing authority of the district but have no other credit enhancement except what the developer may be required to provide in certain situations. The developer uses the proceeds to pay for on-site utilities such as water lines, sewer lines, drainage improvements, fire hydrants and manholes and for off-site facilities such as treatment plants and pipe lines that connect the subdivision to off-site facilities. (p. 26)

They continue: "MUDs are governed by a board of five directors appointed initially by the Texas Water Rights Commission *on the recommendation of the developer*" (p. 26; emphasis added).

11. Perrenod, *Special Districts, Special Purposes*, p. 21; Stark, "Patterns of Legislator Incumbency in Independent Taxing Non-School Special Districts of California," p. 37.

12. Mike McCarthy, "Bond Issue Readied to Buy Laguna Infrastructure," *The Business Journal—Sacramento*, May 11, 1987, v. 4, n. 6, sec. 1, p. 9; emphasis added.This picture of developer initiation and interest in special districts is supported by additional evidence. For example, when the Hamilton Creek Metropolitan District in Colorado went bankrupt in January, 1990, the major consequence noted in the newspaper story about the proceedings was that reorganization was critical "if the developer, Blackmun & Co., is to sell additional lots" ("'Precedent-setting' municipal bankruptcy case receives final court approval," Business Wire, January 5, 1990, dateline, Denver). An article on the 1984 defeat of Proposition 36 noted that the proposal would have eliminated the possibility of publicly funded infrastructure for new development, funding that generally comes through special districts. A senior partner in Cox, Castle & Nicholson, a Los Angeles–based real estate law firm, noted that due to the defeat, "Developers will be free to build new residential tracts without worrying about

how to pay for new schools, police and fire stations, and parks" ("Developers to Benefit by Defeat of Prop. 36," PR Newswire, November 7, 1984, dateline, Los Angeles). And a recent study notes:

> Of particular interest to developers, special districts are being formed to finance infrastructure improvements that support new development, including water and sewer services and road improvements. (Porter, "Financing Infrastructure with Special Districts," p. 10)

This same study points out that the money to finance infrastructure can come from one of two sources: developers or special districts (p. 11).

13. Bollens, "Examining the Link Between State Policy and the Creation of Local Special Districts," p. 119; Perrenod, *Special Districts, Special Purposes*, p. 23.

14. Porter, Lin, and Peiser, *Special Districts*, p. 19.

15. Porter, Lin, and Peiser, *Special Districts*, p. 19.

16. Porter, Lin, and Peiser, *Special Districts*, p. 22.

17. Scott Miller, "So. King Lament: 'Country Road, Take Me Home . . .'," *Puget Sound Business Journal*, August 31, 1987, v. 8, n. 16, sec. 1, p. 17. See Mike McCarthy, "Roseville Sells Its Bonds for Olympus Infrastructure Job," *The Business Journal—Sacramento*, May 23, 1988, v. 5, n. 8, sec. 1, p. 2, for a discussion of one instance where special districts reimbursed a developer for $27.38 million in infrastructure improvements.

18. Porter, Lin, and Peiser, *Special Districts*, p. 20.

19. "These Businesses Tax Themselves: In the Cumberland-Galleria Area, Businesses Formed a Tax District to Cope with Rapid Growth," *Georgia Trend*, January 1989, v. 4, n. 5, sec. 1, p. 17.

20. Lisa Jennings, "Damn This Traffic Jam (It Hurts My Motor to Go So Slow)," *Washington Business Journal*, July 1987, sec. 1., p. 32.

21. Samuel P. Hays, *Conservation and the Gospel of Efficiency: The Progressive Conservation Movement, 1890–1920* (Cambridge: Harvard University Press, 1959), pp. 223, 225.

22. For an argument about institutions that enforce cooperation, see Elinor Ostrom, *Governing the Commons* (Cambridge: Cambridge University Press, 1990).

23. John Portz, *The Politics of Plant Closings* (Lawrence: University Press of Kansas, 1990), p. 85.

24. Portz, *The Politics of Plant Closings*, p. 85.

25. Portz, *The Politics of Plant Closings*, p. 96.

26. The Census of Governments Government Organization Data File is the source of information about whether districts have employees.

27. Bowen, "Reshaping Special District Government in Arizona."

28. A recent *Industry Week* article notes that "the number of special districts is growing, which suggests continued rising demand for such items as autos,

mowers, and telecommunications gear." See "Government's Shopping List," *Industry Week*, February 20, 1989, p. 80.

29. Ernest S. Griffith, *A History of American City Government: The Conspicuous Failure, 1870–1900* (New York: Praeger, 1974), p. 154.

30. The following discussion of the formation of the Metropolitan Water District of Southern California is drawn from Vincent Ostrom, *Water and Politics* (Los Angeles: The Haynes Foundation, 1952), pp. 171–97.

31. Arthur Maass and Raymond L. Anderson, . . . *and the Desert Shall Rejoice* (Cambridge: MIT Press, 1978).

Maass and Anderson note similarly that the formation of California irrigation districts occurred as canal companies were floundering financially because they could not force landowners whose land abutted land irrigated by the company (and who benefitted by the rising water table) to pay for the benefits of irrigation. Many of the districts were formed in the early 1900s; they purchased the canal companies, paid off their debt, and operated the irrigation systems from then on in California. According to Maass and Anderson, the organizational force seems to have been the farmers themselves, although the picture is vague at best. As with the formation of the Southern California water district, these districts were useful because they could finance projects, but they were also useful because they could eliminate free riders.

32. F. Lee Brown and Helen M. Ingram, *Water and Poverty in the Southwest* (Tucson: University of Arizona Press, 1987); Helen M. Ingram, *Water Politics: Continuity and Change* (Albuquerque: University of New Mexico Press, 1990); John Nichols, "To Save a Dying Culture," *Race Relations Reporter* 5(July 1974):20–24.

33. The following discussion is based upon Nichols, "To Save a Dying Culture." A fictionalized account of the following formation effort is presented in John Nichols, *The Milagro Beanfield War* (New York: Holt, Rinehart, and Winston, 1974).

34. Nichols, "To Save a Dying Culture."

35. Nichols, "To Save a Dying Culture," p. 21.

36. Nichols, "To Save a Dying Culture," p. 21, quoting from Middle Rio Grande Regional Conservator Hugh Calkins' 1936 study, *A Reconnaissance Survey of Human Dependency on Resources in the Rio Grande Watershed*.

37. Nichols, "To Save A Dying Culture," p. 22.

38. Brown and Ingram, *Water and Poverty in the Southwest*, p. 62.

39. Richard E. Foglesong, "Do Politics Matter in the Formulation of Local Development Policies? The Orlando–Disney World Relationship," paper prepared for delivery at the 1989 Annual Meeting of the American Political Science Association. Atlanta, GA, August 31–September 3, 1989, p. 14.

40. Foglesong, "Do Politics Matter in the Formulation of Local Development Policies?" p. 16.

41. Foglesong, "Do Politics Matter in the Formulation of Local Development Policies?"

42. Kevin R. Cox and Frank F. Nartowicz, "Jurisdictional Fragmentation in the American Metropolis," *International Journal of Urban and Regional Research* 4(June, n.2, 1980):203.

43. Interestingly, Miller notes in his study of the formation of the Lakewood Plan cities that no one he interviewed "was able to point to differences in preferences for public services" (Miller, *Cities by Contract*, p. 62).

44. Teaford, *City and Suburb*, pp. 26–7.

45. Teaford, *City and Suburb*, p. 6.

46. Illinois, 1831; Pennsylvania, 1834; Arkansas and New York, 1837; Iowa, 1847; Wisconsin, 1849; Tennessee and California, 1850; Michigan, 1857.

47. Kathleen Underwood, *Town Building on the Colorado Frontier* (Albuquerque: University of New Mexico Press, 1987), pp. 9–12.

48. Underwood, *Town Building on the Colorado Frontier*, p. 51.

49. Kenneth T. Jackson and Stanley K. Schultz, *Cities in American History* (New York: Alfred A. Knopf, 1972), p. 106.

50. Kenneth Marvin Hamilton, *Black Towns and Profit: Promotion and Development in the Trans-Appalachian West, 1877–1915*, (Urbana: University of Illinois Press, 1991), pp. 149–152. The quotation is from p. 152.

51. Kenneth A. Lockridge, *Settlement and Unsettlement in Early America* (Cambridge: Cambridge University Press, 1981), p. 41.

52. Lockridge, *Settlement and Unsettlement in Early America*, pp. 40, 41.

53. Paul Boyer and Stephen Nissenbaum, *Salem Possessed: The Social Origins of Witchcraft* (Cambridge: Harvard University Press, 1974), chapter 2, and in particular, pp. 39–59. I am grateful to Gerald Gamm for telling me about this case.

54. See also Jon Teaford, *The Twentieth-Century American City* (Baltimore: Johns Hopkins University Press), p. 107.

55. Historians—Binford and Monkkonen, in particular—have begun recently to reconsider traditional explanations for why municipalities, and suburbs in particular, formed in the 1800s. In Monkkonen's words: "it is clear that American cities are definitely not 'natural'" (Eric H. Monkkonen, *America Becomes Urban: The Development of U.S. Cities and Towns, 1780–1980*, Berkeley: University of California Press, 1988). And in Binford's words:

> too much twentieth-century thinking about suburbs rests on a narrow and teleological conception of their origins. American city watchers, fascinated for more than a century by repeated cycles of suburban growth, have lost sight of the first stages in the process and never paid much attention to what was there before. (Henry C. Binford, *The First Suburbs: Residential Communities on the Boston Periphery, 1815–1860*, Chicago: University of Chicago Press, 1985, p. 3)

Their arguments, too, focus more explicitly upon the role of businesses in structuring local government even in the early years of suburbanization.

56. James Jose Raigoza, "The Ad Hoc Committee to Incorporate East Los Angeles" (unpublished Ph.D. dissertation. University of California–Los Angeles, 1977), pp. 60–4; Macias, Flores, Figueroa, and Aragon, *A Study of Unincorporated East Los Angeles.*

57. Teaford, *City and Suburb.*

58. See the discussions in Wood, *1400 Governments*, p. 56; Kenneth T. Jackson, *Crabgrass Frontier* (New York: Oxford University Press, 1985), pp. 241, 287; Danielson, *The Politics of Exclusion*; Eric Schmitt, "Home Rule Slips in New York as Region Tackles Big Issues," *New York Times*, August 10, 1989, pp. A1, B4; Robert Huckfeldt, *Politics in Context* (New York: Agathon Press, 1986), p. 153; Eric W. Bond and N. Edward Coulson, "Externalities, Filtering, and Neighborhood Change," *Journal of Urban Economics* 26 (1989):231–49.

59. Sumner Chilton Powell, *Puritan Village: The Formation of a New England Town* (Middletown, CT: Wesleyan University Press, 1963), p. 52.

60. Powell, *Puritan Village*, p. 92.

61. Powell, *Puritan Village*, p. 94.

62. Powell, *Puritan Village*, p. 94.

63. Powell, *Puritan Village*, p. 134.

64. Powell, *Puritan Village*, p. 175.

65. Edward Channing, *Town and County Government in the English Colonies of North America* (Baltimore: Johns Hopkins University Studies in Historical and Political Science, second series, vol. X, 1884), p. 47.

66. Teaford, *City and Suburb*, p. 23.

67. Danielson, *The Politics of Exclusion*, p. 31.

68. Danielson, *The Politics of Exclusion*, p. 31.

69. Danielson, *The Politics of Exclusion*, p. 31–33.

70. George Muller, *Exclusionary Zoning* (Austin: Bureau of Government Research, University of Texas at Austin, 1972), pp. 23, 32; Jerome G. Rose, *Legal Foundations of Land Use Planning* (New Brunswick, NJ: Center for Urban Policy Research, Rutgers, 1974). Rose argues that "In spite of the differences between racial and economic imbalance, it seems very clear, as the Supreme Court has observed, that evidence is available to show that discrimination against low-income groups is, to a large extent, discrimination against racial minorities" (p. 150).

71. Wiliam Glaberson, "Orthodox Jews Battle Neighbors in a Zoning War," *New York Times*, June 3, 1991, pp. A1, B12.

72. Miller (*Cities by Contract*, p. 35) argues that these motivations are too vague to be related in any systematic way to incorporation. For the other side of the argument see Teaford, *City and Suburb*, p. 17; Robert M. Fogelson, *The Fragmented Metropolis: Los Angeles, 1850–1930* (Cambridge: Harvard Uni-

versity Press, 1967), p. 274 and passim. For an interesting twist on this theme, see Elizabeth Kolbert, "Hasidic Village Wants Own Public School District," *New York Times,* July 21, 1989, pp. A1, B4; "Incorporate? Yes or No," *Pahrump Valley Times,* Nye County, CA, v. 21, n. 12, March 23, 1990, p. 1.

73. Jackson, *Crabgrass Frontier,* p. 151; emphasis added.

74. Joanne Ball, "For Many, Mandela Bid Lacks Fire of '86," *Boston Globe,* October 5, 1988, p. 33.

75. Roger House, "Mandela Referendum: Blacks in Boston Seek to Secede," *The Nation,* November 7, 1988, v. 247, n. 13, p. 452.

76. Ball, "For Many, Mandela Bid Lacks Fire of '86," p. 33.

For different reasons, Malibu, California, also sought local control in 1976 and again in 1988. The incorporation movement was opposed by the two largest landowners within the proposed municipal boundaries—the Los Angeles Athletic Club and Pepperdine University, which were worried about, in an official from Pepperdine's words, "economic viability," and in the words of officials from the Athletic Club, "economic uncertainty."

Kenneth J. Garcia, "Lawyer Says Cityhood Would Not Cause Liability Problem for Malibu," *Los Angeles Times,* March 17, 1988, part 9, p. 1; Kenneth J. Garcia, "Pepperdine, Athletic Club Opposed to Malibu Cityhood," *Los Angeles Times,* February 18, 1988, part 9, p. 1.

77. Teaford, *City and Suburb.*

78. Miller, *Cities by Contract;* Teaford, *City and Suburb,* p. 12. See Urban Studies Center, "Annexation, Incorporation, and Consolidation in the Portland Metropolitan Area" (Portland: Urban Studies Center, Portland State College, 1968), p. 1, which argues that incorporations in the Portland metropolitan area have "been used primarily to prevent annexation, zone changes or freeways." Significantly, they report that "incorporation activists feared annexation because they thought it meant a steep rise in tax levies" (Urban Studies Center, "Annexation, Incorporation, and Consolidation in the Portland Metropolitan Area," p. 15).

Annexation, it should be noted, is a common phenomenon. "Almost one-third of the incorporated places with a population of 2,500 or more annex territory each year" (Joel C. Miller, "Municipal Annexation and Boundary Change," *The Municipal Yearbook, 1988,* Washington, DC: International City Managers' Association, 1988, p. 60).

79. Martin, however, provides evidence concerning the lack of typicality of the Lakewood Plan contract cities. She notes, "Between 1954 and 1963, 27 of the 28 new incorporations in Los Angeles County were contract cities. Eight other counties [in California] have at least one contract city which they provide with municipal services" (Martin, "The Institutional Framework of Community Formation," p. 76).

A study of annexation activity in the 1950s finds that the best predictor of annexation activity is the stringency of annexation laws in the state (David G. Bromley, "The Significance of the Annexation Process in Metropolitan Areas of the United States: 1840–1960," unpublished Ph.D. dissertation, Drake University, 1971).

80. Miller, *Cities by Contract*, pp. 42–43.

81. Miller, *Cities by Contract*, p. 45.

82. Miller, *Cities by Contract*, pp. 49, 50.

83. Miller, *Cities by Contract*, p. 52.

84. Miller, *Cities by Contract*, pp. 19–20.

85. Miller, *Cities by Contract*, p. 18.

86. Miller, *Cities by Contract*, pp. 18–19.

87. Miller, *Cities by Contract*, pp. 19–20.

88. Miller, *Cities by Contract*, p. 20.

89. Miller argues, however, that these successes were not imposed from above, but that instead the citizens "behaved very much like cool, calculating economic actors . . . the prevalence of rational calculation was striking . . . it was meaningful only in the context of economic incentives" (Miller, *Cities by Contract*, p. 33). Miller argues that annexation movements succeed where it is in the economic interests of citizens to allow them to succeed.

90. Miller, *Cities by Contract*, p. 13.

91. Arnold Fleischmann, "The Politics of Annexation: A Preliminary Assessment of Competing Paradigms," *Social Science Quarterly* 67(March 1986):138.

92. UPI Press Release, June 10, 1985, BC cycle, Regional News for Arizona and Nevada, dateline, Tucson.

93. Levittown Civic Association, "A Study of the Factors Involved in the Incorporation of Levittown, Bucks County, PA."

94. Gilberto Rafael Cruz, *Let There Be Towns: Spanish Municipal Origins in the American Southwest, 1610–1810* (College Station: Texas A & M University Press, 1988), p. 89 and passim.

95. Cruz, *Let There Be Towns*, p. 77.

96. Charles Hoch, "Municipal Contracting in California: Privatizing with Class," *Urban Affairs Quarterly* 20(March, n.3, 1985):309.

97. Arnold Fleischmann, "The Goals and Strategies of Local Boundary Changes," *Journal of Urban Affairs* 8(Fall, n.4, 1986):67. Hoch argues that industrial interests want lower production costs and commercial interests want better control of their markets. These interests are successful, he argues, because of the bias toward capital in the incorporation process in California. The following table documents the success of these interests, at least in Los Angeles County, between 1950 and 1963 (Charles Hoch, "City Limits: Municipal Boundary Formation and Class Segregation," in William K. Tabb and Larry Sawyers, eds., *Marxism and the Metropolis*, 2nd ed., New York: Oxford University Press, 1984, pp. 101–19). Others have noted the difficulty of forming a municipality:

Only half of the attempts to incorporate areas around San Antonio, Texas, between 1939 and 1986 succeeded (Arnold Fleischmann, "The Politics of Annexation: A Preliminary Assessment of Competing Paradigms," *Social Science Quarterly* 67 [March 1986]:138).

Successful Percentage of Incorporation Attempts in the San Gabriel Region, 1950–63

| | Organization Attempting | | |
	Homeowner	Chamber	Industrial
Start	100%	100%	100%
Petition	5%	66%	100%
Hearing	5%	66%	100%
Implementation	5%	38%	100%
N	21	21	4

Source: Hoch, "City Limits: Municipal Boundary Formation and Class Segregation," p. 109.

98. Jon C. Teaford, *The Municipal Revolution in America: Origins of Modern Urban Government, 1650–1825* (Chicago: University of Chicago Press, 1975), p. 17. It is unclear, however, how committed Penn was to granting municipalities the power to carry out these goals: "Philadelphia's city corporation seems to have restricted its activities to hosting visiting dignitaries and supervising the markets, fairs, and wharves" (Monkkonen, *America Becomes Urban*, p. 112). See also Sam Bass Warner, *The Private City*, 2nd ed. (Philadelphia: University of Pennsylvania Press, 1987), p. 9.

99. Monkkonen, *America Becomes Urban*, p. 122

100. Teaford, *City and Suburb*.

101. Teaford, *City and Suburb*, p. 14.

102. Miller, *Cities by Contract*, p. 33.

103. Janice L. Sperow, "Rajneeshpuram: Religion Incorporated," *Hastings Law Journal* 36(1985):926.

104. Sperow, "Rajneeshpuram," p. 928.

105. Sperow, "Rajneeshpuram," p. 931.

106. Kolbert, "Hasidic Village Wants Own Public School District," pp. A1, B4.

107. Miller, *Cities by Contract*, p. 91.

108. Teaford, *City and Suburb*.

109. Robert J. Waste, "The Early Years in the Life Cycle of City Councils," *Urban Studies* 20(1983):75.

Chapter 3

1. James E. Cooley, *Recollections of Early Days in Duluth* (Duluth, 1925), p. 19, quoted in Eric Monkkonen, "The Politics of Municipal Indebtedness and Default, 1850–1936," in Terrence J. McDonald and Sally K. Ward, eds., *The Politics of Urban Fiscal Policy* (Beverly Hills: Sage, 1984), p. 135.

2. Statute quoted in Henry Wade Rogers, "Municipal Corporations," in *Two Centuries' Growth of American Law, 1701–1901* (New York: Charles Scribner's Sons, 1901), pp. 222–3.

3. Clearly, people may have lived near each other for the additional purpose of defense.

4. Carville Earle and Ronald Hoffman, "The Urban South: The First Two Centuries," in Blaine A. Brownell and David R. Goldfield, eds., *The City in Southern History* (Port Washington, NY: Kennikat Press, 1977), pp. 23–4. See, too, the excellent discussion in Richard E. Fogelsong, *Planning the Capitalist City* (Princeton: Princeton University Press, 1986).

5. See the discussions of local autonomy and local functions in Bruce C. Daniels, *Town and County: Essays on the Structure of Local Government in the American Colonies* (Middletown, CT: Wesleyan University Press, 1978).

6. David J. Rothman, *The Discovery of the Asylum: Social Order and Disorder in the New Republic*, rev. ed. (Boston: Little, Brown, 1990), p. 24.

7. Rothman, *The Discovery of the Asylum*, pp. 24–5.

8. Bruce C. Daniels, "The Political Structure of Local Government in Colonial Connecticut," in Daniels, ed., *Town and County*, p. 58.

9. Rothman, *The Discovery of the Asylum*, p. 46.

10. Howard Lee McBain, *The Law and the Practice of Municipal Home Rule* (New York: Columbia University Press, 1916), p. 59. McBain also notes that local political cliques were using these districts to maintain control over services and money in the face of electoral defeats.

11. David Thomas Konig, "The Origins of Local Government in Northern Massachusetts," in Daniels, ed., *Town and County*, p. 14.

12. Lois Green Carr, "The Foundations of Social Order: Local Government in Colonial Maryland," in Daniels, ed., *Town and County*, p. 95.

13. Judith M. Diamondstone, "The Government of Eighteenth-Century Philadelphia," in Daniels, ed., *Town and County*, pp. 250–4; Stetzer, *Special Districts in Cook County*, p. 13.

14. Rothman, *The Discovery of the Asylum*, pp. 172, 186, 204. Rothman argues that settlement laws were less enforceable with the advent of railroad transportation and with increases in population. A number of states—New York, Rhode Island, Connecticut, and Illinois, for example—altered their laws in the face of the increasing difficulty of moving potential residents to their previous residences.

15. See the excellent discussion in Monkkonen, *American Becomes Urban*. As late as 1849, the Wisconsin state legislature discussed the role of fence viewers (*Journal of the Assembly*, Madison, WI: D.T. Dickson, State Printer, 1849). See Henry Wade Rogers, "Municipal Corporations," in *Two Centuries' Growth Of American Law, 1701–1901* (New York: Charles Scribner's Sons, 1901). Rogers notes:

> In 1800 Philadelphia was regarded as the first and most populous city in the United States, its inhabitants numbering seventy thousand. Its streets were paved and partly drained. The city was supplied with water in wooden pipes. It was then the best-lighted town in America. New York City contained sixty thousand people, was badly paved, and undrained. It had no day police. Boston had not become a city, although it had a population of twenty-five thousand. Its streets and sidewalks were alike paved with round cobblestones, the carriageway being separated from the footway by posts and a gutter. The streets were practically unlighted, except as here and there a few oil lamps shed a feeble light upon the darkness. It had no police force worth mentioning. (pp. 218–19)

See Stanley K. Schultz, *Constructing Urban Culture* (Philadalphia: Temple University Press, 1989).

16. Milo Roy Maltbie, "Municipal Functions: A Study of the Development, Scope and Tendency of Municipal Socialism," *Municipal Affairs* 2(n.4, December 1898):725.

17. Maltbie, "Municipal Functions," p. 735. When Lynchburg, Virginia, installed gas lighting in 1851, the local newspaper remarked:

> The mere fact that a town is lit with gas . . . is an assurance to a stranger that there is an intelligent enterprising and thrifty people, that understands its interests, appreciates the blessings of a well-organized government and is not forgetful of the comforts of home. It is a passport to public confidence and respect, a card to be admitted into the family of well-regulated cities. (David R. Goldfield, "Pursuing the American Urban Dream: Cities in the Old South," in Brownell and Goldfield, eds., *The City in Southern History*, p. 76)

18. Maltbie, "Municipal Functions," p. 735.

19. Maltbie, "Municipal Functions," p. 738.

20. Seymour I. Toll, *Zoned American* (New York: Grossman Publishers, 1969), p. 51.

21. Maltbie, "Municipal Functions," p. 743.

22. Maltbie, "Municipal Functions," p. 704.

23. Joan C. Williams, "The Constitutional Vulnerability of American Local Government," *Wisconsin Law Review* (1986):142; Michael Monroe Kellogg Sebree, "One Century of Constitutional Home Rule," *Washington Law Review* 64(January 1989):156.

24. Annmarie Hauck Walsh, *The Public's Business: The Politics and Practices of Government Corporations* (Cambridge: MIT Press, 1978), p. 19.

25. Walsh, *The Public's Business*, p. 18.

26. Monkkonen,*America Becomes Urban*, p. 138. One early use of municipal bonds was to fund the construction of highways; by 1825, states and municipalities provided most of the funding for their construction (Walsh, *The Public's Business*, p. 17). Philadelphia floated bonds for its gas works in the mid-1800s (Laurence Stevens Knappen, *Revenue Bonds and the Investor*, New York: Prentice-Hall, 1939, p. 7).

27. Monkkonen, *America Becomes Urban*, p. 146.

28. Maass and Anderson, . . . *and the Desert Shall Rejoice*, pp. 173, 175.

29 See Knappen, *Revenue Bonds and the Investor*, chapter 9, for a discussion of some turn-of-the century enabling legislation.

30. Council of State Governments, *Public Authorities in the States* (Chicago: Council of State Governments, 1953), p. 19.

31. Council of State Governments, *Public Authorities in the States*, p. 19.

32. Knappen, *Revenue Bonds and the Investor*, pp. 16–17.

33. See, for example, William Anderson, *The Law of Special Legislation and Municipal Home Rule in Minnesota* (Minneapolis: University of Minnesota Press, 1923).

34. Griffith, *A History of the American City*.

35. Joseph D. McGoldrick, *Law and Practice of Municipal Home Rule, 1916–1930* (New York: Columbia University Press, 1933), pp. 3–4.

36. McBain, *The Law and the Practice of Municipal Home Rule*, p. 67.

37. McBain, *The Law and the Practice of Municipal Home Rule*, p. 67.

38. Thomas C. Devlin, *Municipal Reform in the United States* (New York: G.P. Putnam's Sons, 1896), quoting from James Bryce, *The American Commonwealth*, v. 1 (London: Macmillan, 1891), pp. 660–1.

39. Eric H. Monkkonen, "The Politics of Municipal Indebtedness and Default, 1850–1936," in Terrence J. McDonald and Sally K. Ward, eds., *The Politics of Urban Fiscal Policy* (Beverly Hills: Sage, 1984), pp. 125–60.

40. Monkkonen, "The Politics of Municipal Indebtedness and Default," p. 138.

41. Monkkonen, "The Politics of Municipal Indebtedness and Default," p. 143.

42. Griffith, *A History of American City Government*, p. 212.

43. Jon Teaford, "Special Legislation and the Cities, 1865–1900," *American Journal of Legal History* 23 (1979):189–212.

44. For a discussion of the various forms of prohibitions on special legislation, see Charles Chauncey Binney, *Restrictions Upon Local and Special Legislation in State Constitutions* (Philadelphia: Kay and Brother, Publishers, 1894). See pp. 156–9 for a discussion of special legislation with regard to municipal incorporation.

45. The legislative journals documenting the passage of general incorpora-

tion legislation are not illuminating; the votes are nearly unanimous, but the nature of the discussion is completely concealed. See, for example, *Journal of the House of Representatives of the State of Michigan* (Lansing, MI: Hosmer and Fitch, 1857), pp. 274, 593; *Journal of the Senate of the State of California at their First Session* (San Jose, CA: J. Winchester, 1849), pp. 857, 871–2, 875, 1026.

46. Clifford W. Patton, *The Battle for Municipal Reform* (Washington, DC: American Council on Public Affairs, 1940).

47. C. Vann Woodward, *Origins of the New South, 1877–1913* (Baton Rouge: Louisiana State University Press, 1951), p. 54.

48. Woodward, *Origins of the New South*, p. 55.

49. Monkkonen, *America Becomes Urban*, p. 121.

50. Dewey W. Grantham, *Southern Progressivism: The Reconciliation of Progress and Tradition* (Knoxville: University of Tennessee Press, 1983), p. 280.

51. Monkkonen, "The Politics of Municipal Indebtedness and Default," pp. 145–6.

52. Many of the prohibitions against special legislation for the creation of special districts and municipalities had been enacted earlier; however, these prohibitions were incorporated into the general prohibitions against special legislation that states enacted. See McBain, *The Law and the Practice of Municipal Home Rule*, passim.

53. *Jackson v. Corey*, 1811, 8 Johns 385, as discussed in Ronald Edward Seavoy, "The Origins of the American Business Corporation, 1784–1855, New York, The National Model" (unpublished Ph.D. dissertation, University of Michigan, 1969), p. 26.

54. Williams, "The Constitutional Vulnerability of American Local Government," p. 88.

55. Williams, "The Constitutional Vulnerability of American Local Government," p. 89.

56. Williams, "The Constitutional Vulnerability of American Local Government," pp. 104, 118–9, points to the many ways in which courts have supported the construction of the realm of local autonomy. By and large, the realm of local autonomy is that of defining who can and cannot live in a particular locality; sometimes, too, it concerns other definitions of citizenship—in particular, who can vote in special district elections.

57. Ernest S. Griffith, *A History of American City Government: The Progressive Years and Their Aftermath, 1900–1920* (Washington, DC: University Press of America, 1983), p. 298.

58. Grantham, *Southern Progressivism*, p. 303.

59. McBain, *The Law and the Practice of Municipal Home Rule*, p. 59.

60. Advisory Commission on Intergovernmental Relations, *The Problem*

of Special Districts in American Government (Washington, D.C.: ACIR, 1964), p. 59.

61. Smith, *Ad Hoc Governments*, pp. 59, 107.

62. For discussions of the dispersal of enabling legislation for soil conservation districts, see David Adlai Adamson, "The Myth and the Means: The American Idealization of Farm Life and Its Relation to the Decentralization of Agricultural Policy" (senior thesis, Harvard University Department of Government, 1981); Robert J. Morgan, *Governing Soil Conservation: Thirty Years of the New Decentralization* (Washington, DC: Resources for the Future, 1965); Donald C. Blaisdell, *Government and Agriculture* (New York: Farrar and Rinehart, Inc., 1940). For a discussion of housing authority enabling legislation, see Martin Meyerson and Edward C. Banfield, *Politics, Planning, and the Public Interest: The Case of Public Housing in Chicago* (Glencoe, IL: Free Press, 1955).

63. Morgan, *Governing Soil Conservation*, p. 39; Blaisdell, *Government and Agriculture*, pp. 120, 121, 172, 173; Adamson, "The Myth and the Means."

64. Basil Rauch, *The History of the New Deal, 1933–1938* (New York: Capricorn Books, 1944), p. 170. Roosevelt had advocated certain kinds of special districts as governor of New York. In his 1932 Annual Message to the Legislature, he pressed the New York legislature to pass enabling legislation for public utility districts (Franklin Delano Roosevelt, *The Public Papers and Addresses of Franklin D. Roosevelt*, v. 1., *The Genesis of the New Deal, 1928– 1932*, New York: Random House, 1938, p. 123). See Bernard Bellush, *Franklin D. Roosevelt as Governor of New York* (New York: Columbia University Press, 1955); Mark I. Gelfand, *A Nation of Cities: The Federal Government and Urban America, 1933–1965* (New York: Oxford University Press, 1975), p. 62.

65. The source of this information is my analysis of the data from the 1987 Census of Governments. See Council of State Governments, 1953, p. 27.

66. See, for example, Edward F. Haas, "The Southern Metropolis, 1940– 1976," in Brownell and Goldfield, eds., *The City in Southern History*, p. 175.

67. Marc A. Weiss, *The Rise of the Community Builders: The American Real Estate Industry and Urban Land Planning* (New York: Columbia University Press, 1987).

68. Of course, other minority groups have also been the targets of exclusion.

69. Herman H. Long and Charles S. Johnson, *People vs. Property: Race Restrictive Covenants in Housing* (Nashville, TN: Fisk University Press, 1947); see Fogelson, *The Fragmented Metropolis*, for a discussion of restrictive covenants in Los Angeles.

70. Long and Johnson, *People vs. Property*, p. 10.

71. Long and Johnson, *People vs. Property*, pp. 39–40, 42.

72. Long and Johnson, *People vs. Property*, p. 58, emphasis added.

73. *Shelley v. Kraemer*, 341 U.S. 1 (1948). See Meyerson and Banfield, *Politics, Planning, and the Public Interest*, p. 107.

74. To be sure, the redlining policies of the Federal Housing Administration could also serve to enforce segregation. See the discussion in Jackson, *Crabgrass Frontier*, chapter 11.

75. Quoted in Toll, *Zoned American*, p. 129.

76. See Toll, *Zoned American*, p. 167 and passim. Police power is the "power to pass laws for the health, safety, order, and general welfare" of the community (p. 168).

77. Toll, *Zoned American*, p. 193. In the legislative journals that included votes on general incorporation legislation, coverage of the debates about zoning is uninformative; see, for example, *Journal of the Senate of the Fifty-first General Assembly of the State of Illinois* (Springfield: Illinois State Journal Company, 1919), pp. 364, 539–40, 562, 1850.

78. Toll, *Zoned American*, p. 194.

79. Toll, *Zoned American*, p. 201.

80. Toll, *Zoned American*, p. 170.

81. Toll, *Zoned American*, p. 227. *Buchanan v. Warley*, 297 Fed. 307, 312–13.

82. Toll, *Zoned American*, p. 242.

83. Bruno Lasker, "The Issue Restated," *Survey* 44(May 22 1920):279. See his earlier statement of this point in Bruno Lasker, "Unwalled Towns," *Survey* 43(March 1920):675–80, 718.

84. The evidence for this claim and for the next two sentences is from my analysis of enabling legislation and special district formation.

Chapter 4

1. Weiss, *The Rise of the Community Builders*; Ned Eichler, *The Merchant Builders* (Cambridge, MA: MIT Press, 1982).

2. Friedland, *Power and Crisis in the City*, p. 62. For a comparison with earlier business location decisions, see Paul Kantor, *The Dependent City* (Glenview, IL: Scott, Foresman, 1988).

3. John H. Mollenkopf, *The Contested City* (Princeton: Princeton University Press, 1983).

4. Mollenkopf, *The Contested City*, p. 27; Edward F. Haas, 1977. "The Southern Metropolis, 1940–1976," in Brownell and Goldfield, eds., *The City in Southern History*, pp. 159–91.

5. Gelfand, *A Nation of Cities*, pp. 157–97.

6. Gelfand, *A Nation of Cities*, p. 303.

7. Gelfand, *A Nation of Cities*, pp. 319–21.

8. Kantor, *The Dependent City*, p. 201.

9. Lawrence D. Brown, James W. Fossett, and Kenneth T. Palmer, eds., *The Changing Politics of Federal Grants* (Washington, DC: Brookings Institution, 1984).

10. Brown, Fossett, and Palmer, *The Changing Politics of Federal Grants*, p. 7.

11. Rozann Rothman, "Changing Expectations of Local Government in Light of the 1960s," in Daniel Elazar, ed., *Cities of the Prairie Revisited* (Lincoln: University of Nebraska Press, 1986), pp. 192–217.

12. Louis Uchitelle, "States and Cities Are Pushing Hard for Higher Taxes," *New York Times*, March 25, 1991, pp. A1, C6.

13. Brown, Fossett, and Palmer, *The Changing Politics of Federal Grants*, p. 28; Timothy Conlan, *New Federalism* (Washington, DC: Brookings Institution, 1988).

14. Kantor, *The Dependent City*, p. 205.

15. Brown, Fossett, and Palmer, *The Changing Politics of Federal Grants*, p. 45.

16. Bernard J. Frieden and Lynne B. Sagalyn, *Downtown, Inc.: How America Rebuilds Cities* (Cambridge: MIT Press, 1989); Eichler, *The Merchant Builders*.

17. Brown, Fossett, and Palmer, *The Changing Politics of Federal Grants*, p. 46.

18. Brown, Fossett, and Palmer, *The Changing Politics of Federal Grants*, p. 49.

19. Gelfand, *A Nation of Cities*, p. 196.

20. Stone, Whelan, and Murin, *Urban Policy and Politics in a Bureaucratic Ages*, pp. 7–8.

21. Mollenkopf, *The Contested City*, p. 28.

22. Aldon D. Morris, *The Origins of the Civil Rights Movement* (New York: Free Press, 1984); Donald R. Matthews and James W. Prothro, *Negroes and the New Southern Politics* (New York: Harcourt, Brace & World, 1966); McAdam, *Political Process and the Development of Black Insurgency, 1930–1970*; Frederick M. Wirt, *Politics of Southern Equality: Law and Social Change in a Mississippi County* (Chicago: Aldine, 1970).

23. See McAdam, *Political Process and the Development of Black Insurgency*, and Matthews and Prothro, *Negroes and the New Southern Politics*.

24. Stone, Whelan, and Murin, *Urban Policy and Politics in a Bureaucratic Age*, pp. 7–8.

25. Gelfand, *A Nation of Cities*, p. 353.

26. See McAdam, *Political Process and the Development of Black Insurgency*.

27. Howard Ball, Dale Krane, and Thomas P. Lauth, *Compromised Compliance: Implementation of the 1965 Voting Rights Act* (Westport, CT: Greenwood Press, 1982), p. 15.

28. Ball, Krane, and Lauth, *Compromised Compliance.*

29. Stone, Whelan, and Murin, *Urban Policy and Politics in a Bureaucratic Age,* p. 8.

30. Stone, Whelan, and Murin, *Urban Policy and Politics in a Bureaucratic Age,* p. 129; Gary Orfield, "Minorities and Suburbanization," in Rachel G. Bratt, Chester Hartman, and Ann Meyerson, eds., *Critical Perspectives on Housing* (Philadelphia: Temple University Press, 1986); Logan and Schneider, "Racial Segregation and Racial Change in American Suburbs, 1970–1980," pp. 874–88.

31. Dennis E. Gale, *Washington: Inner-City Revitalization and Minority Suburbanization* (Philadelphia: Temple University Press, 1987), p. 114; Mark Baldassare, *Trouble in Paradise* (New York: Columbia University Press, 1986), p. 171; Logan and Schneider, "Racial Segregation and Racial Change in American Suburbs, 1970–1980."

32. Gale, *Washington,* p. 114.

33. Gale, *Washington,* p. 111.

34. Logan and Schneider, "Racial Segregation and Racial Change in American Suburbs, 1970–1980."

35. William Julius Wilson, *The Declining Significance of Race,* 2nd ed. (Chicago: University of Chicago Press, 1980). For information about African-American suburbanization in the 1970s, see Logan and Schneider, "Racial Segregation and Racial Change in American Suburbs, 1970–1980."

36. Orfield, "Minorities and Suburbanization."

37. See Orfield, "Minorities and Suburbanization."

38. A better option would be to divide the analyses by the major changes I have just noted. One analysis would be of cities until 1954. One would be of city formation after 1954. One would look at city formation from 1960 until 1965. Another would look at city formation after the passage of the Voting Rights Act. Unfortunately, some of the major variables in the following analyses are available only by decade.

39. Clearly, there are two sources of error in the dependent variable: (a) some governments did not report formation dates and (b) it is possible that some of the governments formed between 1950 and 1987 had dissolved by the time of the 1987 census. There is no reason to believe that missing data should be correlated with the dependent variable, so the first problem should not cause biases in the estimates. On the second point, we would not expect more than a handful of governments in these 200 counties to have both formed and dissolved since 1950. Moreover, the alternative sources of data would have more difficulties than this one. The other sources of data are the printed *Government Organization* volumes, which report the number of governments of each kind present in a county in a particular decade. One could subtract, for example, the number of municipalities in 1952 from the number in 1962 to measure the number of formations in the 1950s. That measure would be more problematic than the one

used here because it would be muddled by dissolutions of governments formed in prior decades.

40. Each of the counties in the United States had an equal probability of being included in the sample.

Chapter 5

1. Maltbie, "Municipal Functions," p. 770.

2. Gregory Weiher, "Public Policy and Patterns of Residential Segregation," *Western Political Quarterly* 42(December 1989):651–77.

3. As Logan and Schneider ("Racial Segregation and Racial Change in American Suburbs") have discussed, the exception here is the South.

4. I also explored whether there were large populations of other minority groups in these new cities. The populations of the other minority groups were the same size as or smaller than the African-American population in these new cities.

5. As I noted above, the number of developers in the county at the beginning of the decade was not available for the 1950s.

6. Ester Fuchs, *Mayors and Money* (Chicago: University of Chicago Press, 1992), argues that the presence of special districts is an important reason why the Chicago city government has less fiscal stress than the New York City government.

7. John C. Rainbolt, "The Absence of Towns in Seventeenth-Century Virginia," in Kenneth Q. Jackson and Stanley K. Schultz, eds., *Cities in American History* (New York: Alfred A. Knopf), 1972, p. 56.

8. Matthew A. Crenson, *The Un-Politics of Air Pollution* (Baltimore: Johns Hopkins University Press, 1971), p. 164.

9. Crenson, *The Un-Politics of Air Pollution*, p. 172.

Chapter 6

1. Andrew D. White in *The Forum*, December 1890, quoted in Teaford, *City and Suburb*, p. 153.

2. Richard Ely, *Taxation in American States and Cities* (New York: Thomas Y. Crowell & Co., 1888), pp. 111, 209. See Stephen Erie, *Rainbow's End*, (Berkeley: University of California Press, 1988), on Connecticut and poll taxes and literacy tests.

3. Stephen L. Elkin, *City and Regime in the American Republic* (Chicago: University of Chicago Press, 1987).

4. Erie, *Rainbow's End*, p. 80.

5. Erie, *Rainbow's End*, pp. 255–7.

6. Erie argues that the timelessness of Peterson's argument causes Peterson to miss the fact that cities can redistribute. See Erie, *Rainbow's End*, pp. 256–7.

7. Paul Peterson, *City Limits* (Chicago: University of Chicago Press, 1981), pp. 105–6.

8. See, for example, the important work of Clarence N. Stone, *Regime Politics: Governing Atlanta, 1946–1988* (Lawrence: University Press of Kansas, 1989). See the collection of articles in John R. Logan and Todd Swanstrom, eds., *Beyond the City Limits: Urban Policy and Economic Restructuring in Comparative Perspective* (Philadelphia: Temple University Press, 1990).

9. Fleischmann, "The Goals and Strategies of Local Boundary Changes," argues for the importance of the fight over boundaries as well.

10. We can think of other approaches to the study of local politics that this perspective could enrich. For example, the city-as-a-growth-machine perspective presented by Logan and Molotch argues that the city is used by land-based interests (largely developers) to increase the exchange value of land. Understanding local politics from this perspective means understanding the arguments between citizens over the relationship between the use value and the exchange value of land within cities. What the perspective developed in this work adds to this growth-machine argument is an additional specification of who wants what from what types of local governments. It points to the divergence between cities and special districts, and suggests that cities have come to be concerned with both use values and exchange values of land because the coalitions that make political success possible in local government contain developers or businesses and other citizens. Citizens, developers, and manufacturers have different interests in local politics. The developers may want cities (and, more likely, special districts) to increase the exchange value of land by providing infrastructure. Manufacturers want cities to keep taxes low and provide minimal services. Citizens want a range of things. They sometimes want citywide insurance concerning the characteristics of their neighbors, they sometimes want services, and they sometimes want low taxes. Americans have given local politics an autonomous space in which to provide all of these things.

11. See Fuchs, *Mayors and Money*, who argues that Chicago's politics are different from New York City's politics, in part, because of Chicago's special districts.

12. Paul Peterson, *City Limits*, argues that development politics frequently happen in the realm of special districts.

13. The results and this perspective also bear upon models of urban politics developed in economics; in particular, the work here can inform economists and political scientists working in the Tiebout tradition. The Tiebout model assumes the process that I explain.

The first part of the Tiebout model assumes that developers provide cities from which residents can choose. By and large, this process has not occurred in this century. Instead, collections of individuals and businesses have provided their own cities. Because the Tiebout model assumes that developers create cities, the model makes problematic the relationship between the first residents of a location (residents whom the model assumes want zoning) and the developer (whose profits would be decreased through the zoning desired by the residents). See Edwin S. Mills and Bruce W. Hamilton, *Urban Economics*, 4th ed. (Glenview, IL: Scott, Foresman, 1989); J. Vernon Henderson, *Economic Theory and the Cities*, 2nd ed. (Orlando: Academic Press, 1985). This is not a problem. Developers create special districts, not cities, at least in this century, and special districts do not zone.

The Tiebout model assumes that cities are simply service-bundle providers. While cities often do provide services, citizens have not created them in order to do that since 1970. The Tiebout model's assumptions are somewhat more accurate for the decade in which it was developed. Nevertheless, even for that decade, the model's assumptions did not encompass the reasons that citizens and entrepreneurs created cities. That cities also provide tax havens and racial exclusion is important. These dimensions would be interesting additions to the model in that they would ground the model more clearly in historical reality.

The research prsented in this work also suggests that citizens are not, as the Tiebout model assumes, interested in zoning simply in order to eliminate free riders from local politics. Citizens are also interested in zoning for its power to exclude African-Americans, not because African-Americans are poor but simply because they are African-Americans. That function is different from simply eliminating free riders and thus carries different weight when it is translated into a normative prescription.

This work also makes problematic the translation of the Tiebout model from municipal politics to special district politics.

14. Elkin, *City and Regime in the American Republic*.

15. For a discussion of how this happens on the national level, see Mark A. Peterson and Jack L. Walker, "Interest Group Responses to Partisan Change: The Impact of the Reagan Administration upon the National Interest Group System," in Allan J. Cigler and Burdett A. Loomis, eds., *Interest Group Politics*, 2nd ed. (Washington, DC: CQ Press, 1986), pp. 162–82.

16. See Paul Schumaker, *Critical Pluralism, Democratic Performance, and Community Power* (Lawrence: University of Kansas Press, 1991), for an excellent discussion of the possibility of democracy in one well-organized college town; Schumaker's study provides the basis for this suggestion.

17. For a discussion of how these politics should contain the possibility of transformative public discussion, see Elkin, *City and Regime in the American Republic*; Alexis de Tocqueville, *Democracy in America* (New York: Vintage,

1835); and Dennis F. Thompson, *John Stuart Mill and Representative Government* (Princeton: Princeton University Press, 1976).

Appendix A

1. Bollens, *Special District Governments in the United States*, p. 17. A UPI release on March 19, 1990, dateline: Santa Fe, New Mexico, reported that the vote to change a special district requirement was thirty-eight to zero.

2. Barbara Pate Glacel, *Regional Transit Authorities* (New York: Praeger, 1983), chapter 2.

3. Bowen, "Reshaping Special District Government in Arizona," p. 19.

4. Chicoine and Walzer, *Governmental Structure and Local Public Finance*, p. 24; Bollens, "Examining the Link Between State Policy and the Creation of Local Special Districts," p. 122.

5. Aronson and Hilley, *Financing State and Local Governments*, p. 78.

6. Delores Tremewan Martin, "The Institutional Framework of Community Formation: The Law and Economics of Municipal Incorporation in California" (unpublished Ph.D. dissertation, Virginia Polytechnic Institute, 1976), p. 8.

7. Martin, "The Institutional Framework of Community Formation," p. 44. While I cannot tell whether this is generalizable, a vote to incorporate a municipality through special legislation in New Mexico—reported by the UPI on March 19, 1981, dateline: Santa Fe, New Mexico—was unanimous.

8. Martin, "The Institutional Framework of Community Formation," p. 44.

9. U.S. Bureau of the Census, *Censur of Governments*, v. 1, n. 4 (Washington: Government Printing Office, 1987), p. 10.

Appendix B

1. See Bernard Weinstein, Harold T. Gross, and John Rees, *Regional Growth and Decline in the United States*, 2nd ed. (New York: Praeger, 1985); Roger W. Schmenner, *Making Business Location Decisions* (Englewood Cliffs, NJ: Prentice-Hall, 1982).

2. See Mark Schneider, "Suburban Fiscal Disparities and the Location Decisions of Firms," *American Journal of Political Science* 29 (August 1985, n.3):587–605.

I should note that I also explored the impact of retail enterprises on the formation of municipalities; they had a small positive effect; however, the coefficients on the retail variables were stasticially insignificant.

3. Ronald C. Fisher, *State and Local Public Finance* (Glenview, IL: Scott,

Foresman, 1988). I also assessed the effects of tax rate limits such as those imposed by California and Massachusetts in recent years. These tax rate limits had no effect upon the formation of either municipalities or special districts. I also explored whether one other aspect of a "good business climate" affected formations—whether the county is in a right-to-work state. Finally, I explored whether debt limits upon local governments affected the formation of either special districts or municipalities. Only tax characteristics mattered.

4. In the initial estimations, I also included a measure for whether the state allowed interlocal service agreements. It desire to achieve interlocal cooperation to solve an areawide problem were a systematic reason for forming special districts, citizens in states that allowed interlocal service agreements should form fewer special districts. This variable, however, was not systematically related to the formation of special districts.

I also assessed whether citizens in states where counties or townships had more powers to provide services formed fewer special districts and cities; the variables for county and township powers had no systematic relationship to the formation of either cities or special districts.

5. I also explored whether the various newly enacted state restrictions upon special district formation (noted in Appendix A) had an effect; they did not. I examined whether who is able to initiate the formation of a special district mattered; in particular, I looked at the extent to which citizens in general (as opposed to government officials) could initiate the process; this variable had no systematic effect. I also considered the effects of minimum population requirements for city formation.

6. I constructed the data set for these analyses from a number of sources. I discuss the data for the dependent variable in the text. I note here the sources of the data for the other variables.

The source of special district enabling laws is my coding of these laws from the compilations of the U.S. Census of Governments from 1952 through 1982. Information on whether municipal incorporation required a special act of the legislature is also from these volumes.

Information on Voting Rights Act coverage is from Ball, Krane, and Lauth, *Compromised Compliance.*

Information on debt and taxing limits is from Coleman, "Government by Special District," and from Merriman, *The Control of Municipal Budgets.*

Information on annexation, interlocal service agreements, and various other state restrictions on local government is from Melvin B. Hill, Jr., *State Laws Governing Local Government Structure and Administration* (Athens: Institute of Government, University of Georgia, 1978); National League of Cities, *Adjusting Municipal Boundaries: Law and Practice* (Washington, DC: National League of Cities, 1966); Bollens, "Examining the Link Between State Policy and the Creation of Local Special Districts"; The League of Virginia Counties, *Laws of the States Relating to Annexation of County Territory* (Charlottesville: League of Virginia Counties, 1950).

Informaiton on corporate taxes is from various issues of the Tax Foundation, *Facts and Figures on Government Finance.*

Information on local business structure is from various issues of the U.S. Bureau of Old Age and Survivors Insurance's (through 1959) and the U.S. Department of Commerce's *County Business Patterns.*

Information on county demographics is from various issues of the U.S. Department of Commerce's *County and City Data Book.*

7. To be sure, governments dissolve, but I would argue that the process that causes governments to dissolve is not just the formation process in reverse.

8. For a more extensive discussion of the Poisson specification, see Gary King, *Unifying Political Methodology* (Cambridge: Cambridge University Press, 1989).

BIBLIOGRAPHY

Adamson, David Adlai. 1981. *The Myth and the Means: The American Idealization of Farm Life and Its Relation to the Decentralization of Agricultural Policy.* Senior thesis. Harvard Government Department.

Adrian, Charles R. 1988. "Forms of City Government in American History." *The Municipal Year Book, 1988.* Washington, DC: International City Managers' Association, pp. 3–12.

Advisory Commision on Intergovernmental Relations. 1964. *The Problem of Special Districts in American Government.* Washington, DC: ACIR.

Advisory Commission on Intergovernmental Relations. 1965. *Factors Affecting Voter Reactions to Governmental Reorganization in Metropolitan Areas.* Washington, DC: ACIR.

Advisory Commission on Intergovernmental Relations. 1971. "Metropolitan America: Some Consequences of Fragmentation." In Charles M. Bonjean, Terry W. Clark, and Robert L. Lineberry, eds. *Community Politics.* New York: Free Press, pp. 51–5.

Advisory Commission on Intergovernmental Relations. 1987. *The Organization of Local Public Economics.* Washington, DC: ACIR.

Alford, Robert R., and Eugene C. Lee. 1968. "Voting Turnout in American Cities." *American Political Science Review* 62(September):796–813.

Allison, Edward P., and Boies Penrose. 1887. *Philadelphia: 1681–1887.* Baltimore: Johns Hopkins University Press.

Almond, Gabriel, and Sidney Verba. 1963. *The Civic Culture.* Boston: Little, Brown.

Anderson, William. 1923. *The Law of Special Legislation and Municipal Home Rule in Minnesota.* Minneapolis, MN: University of Minnesota.

Aronson, J. Richard, and John L. Hilley. 1987. *Financing State and Local Governments,* 4th ed. Washington, DC: The Brookings Institution.

Baldassare, Mark. 1986. *Trouble in Paradise.* New York: Columbia University Press.

Baldassare, Mark. 1989. "Citizen Support for Regional Government in the New Suburbia." *Urban Affairs Quarterly* 24(March, n.3):460–9.

Ball, Howard, Dale Krane, and Thomas P. Lauth. 1982. *Compromised Compliance: Implementation of the 1965 Voting Rights Act.* Westport, CT: Greenwood Press.

Ball, Joanne. 1988. "For Many, Mandela Bid Lacks Fire of '86." *Boston Globe.* October 5, p. 33.

Banfield, Edward C. 1970. *The Unheavenly City*. Boston: Little, Brown.

Banfield, Edward C., and James Q. Wilson. 1963. *City Politics*. Cambridge: Harvard University Press.

Bellush, Bernard. 1955. *Franklin D. Roosevelt as Governor of New York*. New York: Columbia University Press.

Binford, Henry C. 1985. *The First Suburbs*. Chicago: University of Chicago Press.

Binford, Henry C. 1988. "The Early Nineteenth-Century Suburb: Creating a Suburban Ethos in Somerville and Cambridge, Massachusetts, 1820–1860." In Daniel Schaffer, ed. *Two Centuries of American Planning*. Baltimore: Johns Hopkins University Press, pp. 41–60.

Bingham, Richard D. 1986. *State and Local Government in an Urban Society*. New York: Random House.

Binney, Charles Chauncey. 1894. *Restrictions upon Local and Special Legislation in State Constitutions*. Philadelphia: Kay and Brother.

Blaisdell, Donald C. 1940. *Government and Agriculture*. New York: Farrar and Rinehart.

Bollens, John C. 1957. *Special District Governments in the United States*. Berkeley: University of California Press.

Bollens, Scott A. 1986. "Examining the Link Between State Policy and the Creation of Local Special Districts." *State and Local Government Review* (Fall):117–24.

Bond, Eric W., and N. Edward Coulson. 1989. "Externalities, Filtering, and Neighborhood Change." *Journal of Urban Economics* 26:231–49.

Bonjean, Charles M., Terry N. Clark, and Robert L. Lineberry. 1971. "The Multiplicity of Local Governments." In Charles M. Bonjean, Terry N. Clark, and Robert L. Lineberry, eds. *Community Politics*. New York: Free Press, pp. 45–9.

Bowen, Don L. 1984. "Reshaping Special District Government in Arizona." *Arizona Review* 32(Winter, n.1):12–25.

Bowman, Ann O'M., and Richard C. Kearney. 1993. *State and Local Government*, 2nd ed. Boston: Houghton Mifflin.

Boyer, Paul, and Stephen Nissenbaum. 1974. *Salem Possessed*. Cambridge: Harvard University Press.

Bridges, Amy. 1984. *A City in the Republic*. Cambridge: Cambridge University Press.

Bromley, David G. 1971. "The Significance of the Annexation Process in Metropolitan Areas of the United States: 1840–1960." Unpublished Ph.D. dissertation. Drake University.

Brown, F. Lee, and Helen M. Ingram. 1987. *Water and Poverty in the Southwest*. Tucson: University of Arizona Press.

Brown, Lawrence D., James W. Fossett, and Kenneth T. Palmer. 1984. *The*

Changing Politics of Federal Grants. Washington, DC: The Brookings Institution.

Brown, M. Craig, and Charles N. Halaby. 1984. "Bosses, Reform, and the Socioeconomic Bases of Urban Expenditure, 1890–1940." In Terrence J. McDonald and Sally K. Ward, eds. *The Politics of Urban Fiscal Policy.* Beverly Hills, CA: Sage, pp. 69–100.

Brownell, Blaine A. 1977. "The Urban South Comes of Age, 1900–1940." In Blaine A. Brownell and David R. Goldfield, eds. *The City in Southern History.* Port Washington, NY: Kennikat Press, pp. 123–58.

Brownell, Blaine A., and David R. Goldfield. 1977. "Southern Urban History." In Blaine A. Brownell and David R. Goldfield, eds. *The City in Southern History.* Port Washington, NY: Kennikat Press, pp. 5–22.

Buehrer, Judi. 1986. "No Exit? After Years of Spinning Its Wheels, the State Faces Major Hurdles in Upgrading Denver's Highway System." *Denver Business* 9(n.2, sec. 1):20.

Bugbee, James M. 1880. *Local Self-Government in England and the United States.* Boston: A. Williams and Co.

Burnett, Alan D. 1984. "The Application of Alternative Theories in Political Geography: The Case of Political Participation." In Peter Taylor and John House, eds. *Political Geography: Recent Advances and Future Directions.* London: Croom Helm, pp. 25–49.

Burns, Nancy. 1990. "Founding Cities and Institutionalizing Politics." *The Urban Politics Newsletter.* December.

Cain, Lois P. 1983. "To Annex or Not? A Tale of Two Towns: Evanston and Hyde Park." *Explorations in Economic History* 20:58–72.

"Calif-Assn-Realtors; Growth Control Measures Dominate November Election, California Association of Realtors Study Shows." 1987. *Business Wire.* November 12. Dateline, Los Angeles.

Cannon, Angie. 1990. "'A New Town Within a City' for Detroiters." *Detroit Free Press and News.* September 30, pp. 1A, 8A.

Carr, Lois Green. 1978. "The Foundations of Social Order: Local Government in Colonial Maryland." In Bruce C. Daniels, ed. *Town and County: Essays on the Structure of Local Government in the American Colonies.* Middletown, CT: Wesleyan University Press, pp. 72–110.

Channing, Edward. 1884. *Town and County Government in the English Colonies of North America.* Baltimore: Johns Hopkins University Press.

Chicoine, David L., and Norman Walzer. 1985. *Governmental Structure and Local Public Finance.* Boston: Oelgeschlager, Gunn, & Hain.

Christenson, James A., and Carolyn E. Sachs. 1980. "The Impact of Government Size and Number of Administrative Units on the Quality of Public Services." *Administrative Science Quarterly* 25(March, n.l):89–101.

"Citizens Deserve Facts, Input." 1989. *The Centre Daily Times.* August 10. State College, Pennsylvania. P. A-10.

Clark, Gordon L. 1984. "A Theory of Local Autonomy." *Annals of the Association of American Geographers* 74(June, n.2):195–208.

Clark, Gordon L. 1985. *Judges and the Cities.* Chicago: University of Chicago Press.

Clark, Terry Nichols, and Lorna Crowley Ferguson. 1983. *City Money.* New York: Columbia University Press.

Cole, G. D. H. 1921. *The Future of Local Government.* London: Cassell and Company.

Coleman, Henry A. 1979. "Government by Special Districts." Unpublished Ph.D. dissertation. Princeton University.

Coleman, James S. 1990. *Foundations of Social Theory.* Cambridge: Harvard University Press.

Conlan, Timothy. 1988. *New Federalism: Intergovernmental Reform from Nixon to Reagan.* Washington, DC: The Brookings Institution.

Council of State Governments. 1953. *Public Authorities in the States.* Chicago: Council of State Governments.

Cox, Gary W. 1987. *The Efficient Secret: The Cabinet and the Development of Political Parties in Victorian England.* Cambridge: Cambridge University Press.

Cox, Kevin R., and Frank F. Nartowicz. 1980. "Jurisdictional Fragmentation in the American Metropolis." *International Journal of Urban and Regional Research* 4(June, n.2):196–211.

Crenson, Matthew A. 1971. *The Un-Politics of Air Pollution.* Baltimore: Johns Hopkins University Press.

Cruz, Gilberto Rafael. 1988. *Let There Be Towns: Spanish Municipal Origins in the American Southwest, 1610–1810.* College Station: Texas A & M University Press.

Daniels, Bruce C. 1978a. "The Political Structure of Local Government in Colonial Connecticut." In Bruce C. Daniels, ed. *Town and Country: Essays on the Structure of Local Government in the American Colonies.* Middletown, CT: Wesleyan University Press, pp. 44–71.

Daniels, Bruce C. 1978b. *Town and County: Essays on the Structure of Local Government in the American Colonies.* Middletown, CT: Wesleyan University Press.

Danielson, Michael N. 1976. *The Politics of Exclusion.* New York: Columbia University Press.

Danielson, Michael N., Alan M. Hershey, and John M. Bayne. 1977. *One Nation, So Many Governments.* Lexington, MA: Lexington Books.

Dealey, James Quayle. 1915. *Growth of American State Constitutions: From 1776 to the End of the Year 1914.* Boston: Gins and Company.

"Developers to Benefit by Defeat of Prop. 36." 1984. *PR Newswire*. November 7. Dateline, Los Angeles.

Devlin, Thomas C. 1896. *Municipal Reform in the United States*. New York: G. P. Putnam's Sons.

Diamondstone, Judith M. 1978. "The Government of Eighteenth-Century Philadelphia." In Bruce C. Daniels, ed. *Town and County: Essays on the Structure of Local Government in the American Colonies*. Middletown, CT: Wesleyan University Press, pp. 238–63.

Earle, Carville, and Ronald Hoffman. 1977. "The Urban South: The First Two Centuries." In Blaine A. Brownell and David R. Goldfield, eds. *The City in Southern History*. Port Washington, NY: Kennikat Press, pp. 23–51.

Eichler, Ned. 1982. *The Merchant Builders*. Cambridge: MIT Press.

Elkin, Stephen. 1987. *City and Regime in the American Republic*. Chicago: University of Chicago Press.

Ely, Richard T. 1888. *Taxation in American States and Cities*. New York: Thomas Y. Crowell & Co.

Ely, Richard T. 1902. *The Coming City*. New York: Thomas Y. Crowell & Co.

Erickson, Robert S., John P. McIver, and Gerald C. Wright, Jr. 1987. "State Political Culture and Public Opinion." *American Political Science Review* 81(September, n.3):797–814.

Erie, Steven P. 1988. *Rainbow's End: Irish-Americans and the Dilemmas of Urban Machine Politics, 1840–1985*. Berkeley: University of California Press.

Erie, Steven P. 1990. "Bringing the Bosses Back In: The Irish Political Machines and Urban Policy Making." *Studies in American Political Development*, v. 4. New Haven: Yale University Press, pp. 269–81.

Fairlie, John A. 1904. "American Municipal Councils." *Political Science Quarterly* 19:334–47.

Fairlie, John A. 1906. "Municipal Codes in the Middle West." *Political Science Quarterly* 21:434–46.

Fairlie, John A. 1914. *Local Government in Counties, Towns and Villages*. New York: Century.

Feeney, Ann Philippa. 1988. "Lobbyists: Who's Looking Out for Small Business?" *Colorado Business* 15(n.2, sec. 1):14.

Fisher, Ronald C. 1988. *State and Local Public Finance*. Glenview: Scott, Foresman.

Fleischmann, Arnold. 1986a. "The Goals and Strategies of Local Boundary Changes." *Journal of Urban Affairs* 8(Fall, n.4):63–76.

Fleischmann, Arnold. 1986b. "The Politics of Annexation: Preliminary Assessment of Competing Paradigms." *Social Science Quarterly* 67(March): 128–42.

Florestano, Patricia S. 1980. "Areawide Government and Multiple Jurisdictions." *Publius* 10(Summer, n.3):77–100.

Florestano, Patricia S., and Vincent L. Marando. 1981. *The States and the Metropolis*. New York: Marcel Dekker.

Fogelson, Robert M. 1967. *The Fragmented Metropolis: Los Angeles, 1850–1930*. Cambridge: Harvard University Press.

Foglesong, Richard E. 1986. *Planning the Capitalist City: The Colonial Era to the 1920s*. Princeton: Princeton University Press.

Foglesong, Richard E. 1989. "Do Politics Matter in the Formulation of Local Development Policies? The Orlando–Disney World Relationship." Paper delivered at the 1989 Annual Meeting of the American Political Science Association. Atlanta, GA. August 31–September 3.

Fox, Kenneth. 1985. *Metropolitan America: Urban Life and Urban Policy in the United States, 1940–1980*. New Brunswick, NY: Rutgers University Press.

Freeman, Edward A. 1882. *An Introduction to American Institutional History*. Baltimore: Johns Hopkins University Press.

Fried, Morton H. 1967. *The Evolution of Political Society*. New York: Random House.

Frieden, Bernard J., and Lynne B. Sagalyn. 1989. *Downtown, Inc.: How America Rebuilds Cities*. Cambridge: MIT Press.

Friedland, Roger. 1983. *Power and Crisis in the City*. London: Macmillan.

Frolich, Norman, Joe A. Oppenheimer, and Oran R. Young. 1971. *Political Leadership and Collective Goods*. Princeton: Princeton University Press.

"From the Professional Stream: Currents and Soundings." 1985. *Public Administration Review* 45(n.4):510–14.

Frug, Gerald E. 1988. *Local Government Law*. St. Paul, MN: West.

Fuchs, Ester R. 1992. *Mayors and Money: Fiscal Policy in New York and Chicago*. Chicago: University of Chicago Press.

Gale, Dennis E. 1987. *Washington: Inner-City Revitalization and Minority Suburbanization*. Philadelphia: Temple University Press.

Garcia, Kenneth J. 1988a. "Lawyer Says Cityhood Would Not Cause Liability Problem for Malibu." *Los Angeles Times*. March 19, part 9, p. 1.

Garcia, Kenneth J. 1988b. "Pepperdine, Athletic Club Opposed to Malibu Cityhood." *Los Angeles Times*. February 18, part 9, p. 1.

Gelfand, Mark I. 1975. *A Nation of Cities: The Federal Government and Urban America, 1933–1965*. New York: Oxford University Press.

Gillette, Clayton P. 1983. "Fiscal Federalism and the Use of Municipal Bond Proceeds." *New York University Law Review* 58(November):1030–83.

Glaberson, William. 1991. "Orthodox Jews Battle Neighbors in a Zoning War." *New York Times*. June 3, pp. A1, B12.

Glacel, Barbara Pate. 1983. *Regional Transit Authorities: A Policy Analysis of Massachusetts*. New York: Praeger.

Goldfield, David R. 1977. "Pursuing the American Urban Dream: Cities in the Old South." In Blaine A. Brownell and David R. Goldfield, eds. *The City in Southern History*. Port Washington, NY: Kennikat Press, pp. 52–91.

Goodnow, Frank J. 1906. "Municipal Home Rule." *Political Science Quarterly* 21:77–90.

Gottdiener, Mark. 1977. *Planned Sprawl*. Beverly Hills, CA: Sage.

Gottdiener, Mark. 1987. *The Decline of Urban Politics*. Newbury Park, CA: Sage.

"Government's Shopping List." 1989. *Industry Week*. February 20, p. 80.

Grantham, Dewey W. 1983. *Southern Progressivism: The Reconciliation of Progress and Tradition*. Knoxville: University of Tennessee Press.

Griffith, Ernest S. 1974. *A History of American City Government: The Conspicuous Failure, 1870–1900*. New York: Praeger.

Griffith, Ernest S. 1983. *A History of American City Government: The Progressive Years and Their Aftermath, 1900–1920*. Washington, DC: University Press of America.

Griffith, Ernest S., and Charles R. Adrian. 1983. *A History of American City Government: The Formation of Traditions, 1775–1870*. Washington, DC: University Press of America.

Gunlicks, Arthur B. 1981. *Local Government Reform and Reorganization*. Port Washington, NY: Kennikat Press.

Haas, Edward F. 1977. "The Southern Metropolis, 1940–1976." In Blaine A. Brownell and David R. Goldfield, eds. *The City in Southern History*. Port Washington, NY: Kennikat Press, pp. 159–91.

Hallman, Howard W. 1977. *Small and Large Together*. Beverly Hills, CA: Sage.

Hamilton, Kenneth Marvin. 1991. *Black Towns and Profit: Promotion and Development in the Trans-Appalachian West, 1877–1915*. Urbana: University of Illinois Press.

Hammond Contemporary World Atlas. 1971. Garden City, NY: Doubleday.

Hancock, John. 1988. "The New Deal and American Planning: The 1930s." In Daniel Schaffer, ed. *Two Centuries of American Planning*. Baltimore: Johns Hopkins University Press, pp. 197–230.

Hawkins, Robert B., Jr. 1976. *Self-Government by District*. Stanford, CA: Hoover Institute Press.

Hays, Samuel P. 1959. *Conservation and the Gospel of Efficiency: The Progressive Conservation Movement, 1890–1920*. Cambridge: Harvard University Press.

Henderson, J. Vernon. 1985. *Economic Theory and the Cities*, 2nd ed. Orlando, FL: Academic Press.

Henderson, J. Vernon, and Yannis M. Ioannides. 1989. "Dynamic Aspects of Consumer Decisions in Housing Markets." *Journal of Urban Economics* 26:212–30.

Hill, Dilys M. 1970. *Participation in Local Affairs*. Harmondsworth, Middlesex, England: Penguin Books.

Hill, Melvin B., Jr. 1978. *State Laws Governing Local Government Structure and Administration*. Athens: Institute of Government, University of Georgia.

Hirschman, Albert O. 1970. *Exit, Voice, and Loyalty*. Cambridge: Harvard University Press.

Hoch, Charles. 1984. "City Limits: Municipal Boundary Formation and Class Segregation." In William K. Tabb and Larry Sawyers, eds. *Marxism and the Metropolis*, 2nd ed. New York: Oxford University Press, pp. 101–19.

Hoch, Charles. 1985. "Municipal Contracting in California: Privatizing with Class." *Urban Affairs Quarterly* 20(March, n.3):303–23.

Hogan, Joan Query. 1988. "Localism, the Unexamined Faith: Informal Governance in Contemporary Small Communities." Unpublished Ph.D. dissertation. University of California–Davis.

Hogue, Kendra. 1989. "Long Leads Library Into 21st Century." *The Business Journal–Portland* 6(March 6, n.2, sec. 1):10.

Holzer, Harry J. 1991. "The Spatial Mismatch Hypothesis: What Has the Evidence Shown?" *Urban Studies* 28(February):105–22.

Hornstein, Dave. 1986. "Sweetening the Deal: Incentives for Local Businesses." *Oakland Business* 4(January, n.1, sec. 1):15. Oakland, MI.

House, Roger. 1988. "Mandela Referendum: Blacks in Boston Seek to Secede." *The Nation* 247(November 7, n.13):452.

Huckfeldt, Robert. 1986. *Politics in Context*. New York: Agathon Press.

"Incorporate? Yes or No." 1990. *Pahrump Valley Times* 21(March 23, n.12):1. Nye County, CA.

Ingram, Helen M. 1990. *Water Politics: Continuity and Change*. Albuquerque: University of New Mexico Press.

Irvins, William M. 1887. "Municipal Government." *Political Science Quarterly* 2:291–312.

Jackson, Alan A. 1973. *Semi-Detached London: Suburban Development, Life and Transport, 1900–39*. London: George Allen & Unwin.

Jackson, Kenneth T., and Stanley K. Schultz. 1972. *Cities in American History*. New York: Alfred A. Knopf.

Jackson, Kenneth T. 1985. *Crabgrass Frontier*. New York: Oxford University Press.

Jacob, Herbert. 1985. "Policy Responses to Crime." In Paul E. Peterson, ed. *The New Urban Reality*. Washington, DC: The Brookings Institution, pp. 225–52.

James, Herman G. 1921. *Local Government in the United States.* New York: D. Appleton and Co.

Jennings, Lisa. 1987. "Damn This Traffic Jam (It Hurts My Motor to Go So Slow)." *Washington Business Journal* (July, sec. 1):32.

Johnston, R. J. 1984. *Residential Segregation, the State and Constitutional Conflict in American Urban Areas.* London: Academic Press.

Jones, Bryan D. 1983. *Governing Urban America.* Boston: Little, Brown.

Journal of the Assembly of Wisconsin. 1849. Madison, WI: D. T. Dickson, State Printers.

Journal of the House of Representatives of the State of Michigan. 1857. Lansing: Hosmer & Fitch.

Journal of the Senate of the Fifty-first General Assembly of the State of Illinois. 1919. Springfield: Illinois State Journal Co.

Journal of the Senate of the State of California at Their First Session. 1849. San Jose: J. Winchester.

Kantor, Paul. 1988. *The Dependent City: The Changing Political Economy of Urban America.* Glenview, IL: Scott, Foresman.

Kantor, Paul. 1990. "The Political Economy of Business Politics in U.S. Cities: A Developmental Perspective." *Studies in American Political Development,* v. 4. New Haven: Yale University Press, pp. 248–68.

Karnig, Albert K., and B. Oliver Walter. 1983. "Decline in Municipal Voter Turnout." *American Politics Quarterly* 11 (October, n.4):491–505.

Katznelson, Ira. 1989. "The Burdens of Urban History: Comment." *Studies in American Political Development* 3:30–50.

King, Gary. 1989. *Unifying Political Methodology: The Likelihood Theory of Statistical Inference.* Cambridge: Cambridge University Press.

Knappen, Laurence Stevens. 1939. *Revenue Bonds and the Investor.* New York: Prentice-Hall.

Knott, Jack H., and Gary J. Miller. 1987. *Reforming Bureaucracy: The Politics of Institutional Choice.* Englewood Cliffs, NJ: Prentice-Hall.

Kolbert, Elizabeth. 1989. "Hasidic Village Wants Own Public School District." *New York Times.* July 21, pp. A1, B4.

Ladd, Helen F., and T. Nicholaus. 1981. *Tax and Expenditure Limitations.* Washington, DC: The Urban Institute.

Ladd, Helen F., and Katharine L. Bradbury. 1988. "City Taxes and Property Tax Bases." *National Tax Journal* 41:503–23.

League of Virginia Counties. 1950. *Laws of the States Relating to Annexation of County Territory.* Charlottesville: League of Virginia Counties.

Levittown Civic Association. 1954. "A Study of the Factors Involved in the Incorporation of Levittown, Bucks County, PA." Levittown, PA: Levittown Civic Association.

Liebert, Roland J. 1976. *Disintegration and Political Action.* New York: Academic Press.

Lindley, Ernest K. 1974 (1934). *Franklin D. Roosevelt: A Career in Progressive Democracy*. New York: Da Capo.

Lineberry, Robert L., and Ira Sharkansky. 1974. *Urban Politics and Public Policy*, 2nd ed. New York: Harper and Row.

Lockridge, Kenneth A. 1981. *Settlement and Unsettlement in Early America: The Crisis of Political Legitimacy Before the Revolution*. New York: Cambridge University Press.

Logan, John R. 1976. "Industrialization and the Stratification of Cities in Suburban Regions." *American Journal of Sociology* 82(n.2):333–48.

Logan, John R., and Harvey L. Molotch. 1987. *Urban Fortunes: The Political Economy of Place*. Berkeley: University of California Press.

Logan, John R., and Mark Schneider. 1981. "The Stratification of Metropolitan Suburbs, 1960–1970." *American Sociological Review* 46(n.2): 175–86.

Logan, John R., and Mark Schneider. 1984. "Racial Segregation and Racial Change in American Suburbs, 1970–1980." *American Journal of Sociology* 89(n.4):874–88.

Logan, John R., and Todd Swanstrom, eds. 1990. *Beyond the City Limits: Urban Policy and Economic Restructuring in Comparative Perspective*. Philadelphia: Temple University Press.

Long, Herman H., and Charles S. Johnson. 1947. *People vs. Property: Race Restrictive Covenants in Housing*. Nashville, TN: Fisk University Press.

Lyons, W. E. 1977. *The Politics of City–County Merger: The Lexington-Fayette County Experience*. Lexington: University Press of Kentucky.

Maass, Arthur, and Raymond L. Anderson. 1978. *. . . and the Desert Shall Rejoice*. Cambridge: MIT Press.

Macias, Reynaldo F., Guillermo Vicente Flores, Donaldo Figueroa, and Luis Aragon. 1973. *A Study of Unincorporated East Los Angeles*. Monograph No. 3. Los Angeles: UCLA, Chicano Studies Center.

Macy, Jesse. 1884. *Institutional Beginnings in a Western State*. Johns Hopkins University Studies in Historical and Political Science, second series, v. 7. Baltimore: Johns Hopkins University Press.

Makielski, S. J., Jr., and David G. Temple. 1967. *Special District Government in Virginia*. Charlottesville: University of Virginia, Institute of Government.

Maltbie, Milo Roy. 1898. "Municipal Functions: A Study of the Development, Scope and Tendency of Municipal Socialism." *Municipal Affairs* 2(December, n.4):577–799.

Mansbridge, Jane J. 1980. *Beyond Adversary Democracy*. New York: Basic Books.

Marsh, Steven. 1988. "Hackstaff Reshapes Venerable Ross Co. for 21st Century." *The Denver Business Journal* 39(n.20, sec. 1):10.

Martin, Dolores Tremewan. 1976. "The Institutional Framework of Community Formation: The Law and Economics of Municipal Incorporation in California." Unpublished Ph.D. dissertation. Virginia Polytechnic Institute.

Martin, Dolores Tremewan, and Richard E. Wagner. 1978. "The Institutional Framework for Municipal Incorporation." *Journal of Law and Economics* 21(October):409–26.

Maser, Steven M. 1985. "Demographic Factors Affecting Constitutional Decisions." *Public Choice* 47:121–62.

Matthews, Donald R., and James W. Prothro. 1966. *Negroes and the New Southern Politics.* New York: Harcourt, Brace & World.

McAdam, Doug. 1982. *Political Process and the Development of Black Insurgency, 1930–1970.* Chicago: University of Chicago Press.

McBain, Howard Lee. 1916. *The Law and the Practice of Municipal Home Rule.* New York: Columbia University Press.

McBain, Howard Lee. 1918. *American City Progress and the Laws.* New York: Columbia University Press.

McBain, Howard Lee. 1922a. "The Legal Status of the American Colonial City." *Political Science Quarterly* 40(June, n.2):177–200.

McBain, Howard Lee. 1922b. "The New York Proposal for Municipal Home Rule." *Political Science Quarterly* 37:655–80.

McCarthy, Mike. 1985. "Residential Building Activity Will Stay the Course." *The Business Journal–Sacramento* 2(December 30, n.39, sec. 2):11.

McCarthy, Mike. 1987. "Bond Issue Readied to Buy Laguna Infrastructure." *The Business Journal–Sacramento* 4(May 11, n.6, sec. 1):9.

McCarthy, Mike. 1988. "Roseville Sells Its Bonds for Olympus Infrastructure Job." *The Business Journal–Sacramento* 5(May 23, n.8, sec. 1):2.

McConnell, Grant. 1966. *Private Power and American Democracy.* New York: Alfred A. Knopf.

McDonald, Terrence J. 1984. "San Francisco: Socioeconomic Change, Political Culture, and Fiscal Politics, 1870–1906." In Terrence J. McDonald and Sally K. Ward, eds. *The Politics of Urban Fiscal Policy.* Beverly Hills, CA: Sage, pp. 39–68.

McDonald, Terrence J. 1989a. "Reply to Professor Katznelson." *Studies in American Political Development* 3(n.1):51–5.

McDonald, Terrence J. 1989b. "The Burdens of Urban History." *Studies in American Political Development* 3(n.1):3–29.

McDonald, Terrence J., and Sally K. Ward. 1984a. "Introduction." In Terrence J. McDonald and Sally K. Ward, eds. *The Politics of Urban Fiscal Policy.* Beverly Hills, CA: Sage, pp. 1–38.

McDonald, Terrence J., and Sally K. Ward, eds. 1984b. *The Politics of Urban Fiscal Policy.* Beverly Hills, CA: Sage.

McFeeley, Neil D. 1978. "Special District Governments: The New Dark Continent Twenty Years Later." *Midwest Review of Public Administration* 2(December, n.4):211–45.

McGoldrick, Joseph D. 1933. *Law and Practice of Municipal Home Rule, 1916–1930*. New York: Columbia University Press.

Meltsner, Arnold J. 1971. *The Politics of City Revenue*. Berkeley: University of California Press.

Merriman, David. 1987. *The Control of Municipal Budgets*. New York: Quorum Books.

Meyerson, Martin, and Edward C. Banfield. 1955. *Politics, Planning, and the Public Interest: The Case of Public Housing in Chicago*. Glencoe, IL: Free Press.

Miller, Gary J. 1981. *Cities by Contract: The Politics of Municipal Incorporation*. Cambridge: MIT Press.

Miller, Gary J. 1985. "Progressive Reform as Induced Institutional Preferences: Comment on the Maser Paper." *Public Choice* 47:163–81.

Miller, Joel C. 1988. "Municipal Annexation and Boundary Change." *The Municipal Yearbook, 1988*. Washington, D.C.: International City Managers' Association, pp. 59–67.

Miller, Scott. 1987. "So King Lament: 'Country Road, Take Me Home . . .'". *Puget Sound Business Journal* 8(August 31, n.16, sec. 1):17.

Mills, Edwin S., and Bruce W. Hamilton. 1989. *Urban Economics*, 4th ed. Glenview, IL: Scott, Foresman.

Moe, Terry M. 1980. *The Organization of Interests*. Chicago: University of Chicago Press.

Moeser, John V., and Rutledge M. Dennis. 1982. *The Politics of Annexation*. Cambridge: Schenkman.

Mollenkopf, John H. 1983. *The Contested City*. Princeton: Princeton University Press.

Molotch, Harvey. 1976. "The City as a Growth Machine: Toward a Political Economy of Place." *American Journal of Sociology* 82(n.2):309–32.

Molotch, Harvey. 1990. "Urban Deals in Comparative Perspective." In John R. Logan and Todd Swanstrom, eds. *Beyond the City Limits*. Philadelphia: Temple University Press, pp. 175–98.

Monkkonen, Eric H. 1984. "The Politics of Municipal Indebtedness and Default, 1850–1936." In Terrence J. McDonald and Sally K. Ward, eds. *The Politics of Urban Fiscal Policy*. Beverly Hills, CA: Sage, pp. 125–60.

Monkkonen, Eric H. 1988. *America Becomes Urban: The Development of U.S. Cities and Towns, 1780–1980*. Berkeley: University of California Press.

Morgan, Robert J. 1965. *Governing Soil Conservation: Thirty Years of the New Decentralization*. Washington, DC: Resources for the Future.

Morlan, Robert L. 1967. "Local Governments: An Embarrassment of Riches." In James W. Fesler, ed. *The 50 States and Their Local Governments*. New York: Alfred A. Knopf, pp. 505–49.

Mowry, Duane. 1895. "Reform and Reformers." *American Magazine of Civics* 7(November):462–5.

Muller, George. 1972. *Exclusionary Zoning*. Austin: Bureau of Government Research, University of Texas at Austin.

Murphy, Michael C. 1989. *How to Buy a Home While You Can Still Afford To*, rev. ed. New York: Sterling.

National Bureau of Economic Research. 1989. "The States Keep Up with the Joneses, Too." *The NBER Digest*. (December):1.

National League of Cities. 1966. *Adjusting Municipal Boundaries: Law and Practice*. Washington, DC: National League of Cities.

Newcomer, Mabel. 1928. "Tendencies in State and Local Finance and Their Relation to State and Local Functions." *Political Science Quarterly* 43(March, n.1):1–31.

Newton, Kenneth. 1978. "Conflict Avoidance and Conflict Suppression: The Case of Urban Politics in the United States." In Kevin R. Cox, ed. *Urbanization and Conflict in Market Societies*. Chicago: Maaronfa Press, pp. 76–93.

Nice, David C. 1983. "An Intergovernmental Perspective on Urban Fragmentation." *Social Science Quarterly* 64(March, n.1):111–18.

Nichols, John. 1974a. *The Milagro Beanfield War*. New York: Holt, Rinehart, and Winston.

Nichols, John. 1974b. "To Save a Dying Culture." *Race Relations Reporter* 51(July):20–4.

North, Douglass C. 1990. *Institutions, Institutional Change, and Economic Performance*. Cambridge: Cambridge University Press.

Oakerson, Ronald J., and Roger B. Parks. 1988. "Citizen Voice and Public Entrepreneurship: The Organization Dynamic of a Complex Metropolitan County." *Publius* 18(Fall):91–112.

Oates, Wallace E. 1972. *Fiscal Federalism*. New York: Harcourt, Brace, Jovanovich.

Olson, Mancur. 1965. *The Logic of Collective Action*. Cambridge: Harvard University Press.

Ordeshook, Peter C. 1986. *Game Theory and Political Theory: An Introduction*. Cambridge: Cambridge University Press.

Orfield, Gary. 1986. "Minorities and Suburbanization." In Rachel G. Bratt, Chester Hartman, and Ann Meyerson, eds. *Critical Perspectives on Housing*. Philadelphia: Temple University Press, pp. 221–9.

Orth, Samuel P. 1903. "The Centralization of Administration in Ohio." *Studies in History, Economics and Public Law* 16(n.3):1–177.

Ostrom, Elinor. 1990. *Governing the Commons: The Evolution of Institutions for Collective Action*. Cambridge: Cambridge University Press.

Ostrom, Vincent. 1953. *Water and Politics*. Los Angeles: Haynes Foundation.

Ostrom, Vincent, Robert Bish, and Elinor Ostrom. 1988. *Local Government in the United States*. San Francisco: Institute for Contemporary Studies.

Ostrom, Vincent, Charles M. Tiebout, and Robert Warren. 1961. "The Organization of Government in Metropolitan Areas." *American Political Science Review* 55(December):831–42.

Ostrowski, Krystoff, and Henry Teune. 1974. "Local Political Systems and General Social Processes." In Terry Nichols Clark, ed. *Comparative Community Politics*. New York: Wiley, pp. 395–404.

Paddison, Ronan. 1983. *The Fragmented State*. New York: St. Martin's Press.

Parks, Roger B., and Ronald J. Oakerson. 1989. "Metropolitan Organization and Governance." *Urban Affairs Quarterly* 5(September, n.1):18–29.

Patton, Clifford W. 1940. *The Battle for Municipal Reform*. Washington, DC: American Council on Public Affairs.

Peirce, Neal R. 1990. "Philadelphia: A 1990s Omen for Cities." *National Journal* 22(September, n.38):2287.

Perin, Constance. 1977. *Everything in Its Place: Social Order and Land Use in America*. Princeton: Princeton University Press.

Perrenod, Virginia Marion. 1984. *Special Districts, Special Purposes*. College Station: Texas A & M University Press.

Petersen, John E. 1981. "The Municipal Bond Market." In Norman Walzer and David L. Chicoine, eds. *Financing State and Local Governments in the 1980s*. Cambridge, MA: Oelgeschlager, Gunn & Hain, pp. 129–42.

Peterson, George E. 1987. "Infrastructure Support for Industrial Policy." In Harvey A. Goldstein, eds. *The State and Local Industrial Policy Question*. Chicago: American Planning Association Planner's Press, pp. 95–104.

Peterson, Mark A., and Jack L. Walker. 1986. "Interest Group Responses to Partisan Change: The Impact of the Reagan Administration upon the National Interest Group System." In Allan J. Cigler and Burdett A. Loomis, eds. *Interest Group Politics*, 2nd ed. Washington, DC: CQ Press.

Peterson, Paul E. 1981. *City Limits*. Chicago: University of Chicago Press.

Peterson, Paul E. 1990–91. "The Rise and Fall of Special Interest Politics." *Political Science Quarterly* 105(Winter, n.4):539–56.

Peterson, Paul E., and Paul Kantor. 1977. "Political Parties and Citizen Participation in English City Politics." *Comparative Politics* 9(2, January):197–217.

Peterson, Paul E., Barry G. Rabe, and Kenneth K. Wong. 1986. *When Federalism Works*. Washington, DC: The Brookings Institution.

Phares, Donald. 1989. "Bigger Is Better, Or Is It Smaller?" *Urban Affairs Quarterly* 25(1, September):5–17.

"Plan Drafted for Re-development of East Detroit." 1990. *The Michigan Daily* 101(October 1, n.18):1–2. Ann Arbor, MI.

Porter, Douglas R. 1987. "Financing Infrastructure with Special Districts." *Urban Land* 46(May, n.5):9–13.

Porter, Douglas R., Ben C. Lin, and Richard B. Peiser. 1987. *Special Districts: A Useful Technique for Financing Infrastructure.* Washington, DC: Urban Land Institute.

Porter, Glenn, and Harold C. Livesay. 1971. *Merchants and Manufacturers: Studies in the Changing Structure of Nineteenth-Century Marketing.* Baltimore: Johns Hopkins University Press.

Portney, Paul R. 1976. *Economic Issues in Metropolitan Growth.* Baltimore: Johns Hopkins University Press.

Portz, John. 1990. *The Politics of Plant Closings.* Lawrence: University Press of Kansas.

Powell, Sumner Chilton. 1963. *Puritan Village.* Middleton, CT: Wesleyan University Press.

"'Precedent-setting' Municipal Bankruptcy Case Receives Final Court Approval." 1990. *Business Wire.* January 5. Dateline, Denver.

"The Prevention of Local Extravagance." 1875. *The Nation* 21(July):21–2.

Rabinowitz, Howard N. 1977. "Continuity and Change: Southern Urban Development, 1860–1900." In Blaine A. Brownell and David R. Goldfield, eds. *The City in Southern History.* Port Washington, NY: Kennikat Press, pp. 92–122.

Raigoza, James Jose. 1977. "The Ad Hoc Committee to Incorporate East Los Angeles." Unpublished Ph.D. dissertation. University of California–Los Angeles.

Rainbolt, John C. 1972. "The Absence of Towns in Seventeenth-Century Virginia." In Kenneth T. Jackson and Stanley K. Schultz, eds. *Cities in American History.* New York: Alfred A. Knopf, pp. 50–66.

Rauch, Basil. 1944. *The History of the New Deal, 1933–1938.* New York: Capricorn Books.

Reinhold, Robert. 1989. "Bringing Jobs and Housing Closer—by Force if Necessary." *New York Times* (Sunday, March 19), p. E5.

Richman, Roger. 1985. "Formal Mediation in Intergovernmental Disputes: Municipal Annexation Negotiations in Virginia." *Public Administration Review* 45(n.4):510–17.

Rigos, Platon N., and Charles J. Spindler. 1988. "Municipal Incorporation and State Statutes: A State Level Analysis." Paper delivered at the Annual Conference of the American Political Science Association. Washington, DC September 1–3, 1988.

Rigos, Platon N., and Charles J. Spindler. 1989. "Municipal Incorporation Activity: Why New Cities Are Created." Paper delivered at the Annual Conference of the American Political Science Association. Atlanta, GA, September 3, 1989.

Rogers, Henry Wade. 1901. "Municipal Corporations." In *Two Centuries' Growth of American Law, 1701–1901*. New York: Charles Scribner's Sons, pp. 203–60.

Roosevelt, Franklin Delano. 1938. *The Public Papers and Addresses of Franklin D. Roosevelt. V. 1. The Genesis of the New Deal, 1928–1932*. New York: Random House.

Rose, Jerome G. 1974. *Legal Foundations of Land Use Planning*. New Brunswick, NJ: Center for Urban Policy Research, Rutgers University Press.

Rothman, David J. 1990. *The Discovery of the Asylum: Social Order and Disorder in the New Republic*, rev. ed. Boston: Little, Brown.

Sbragia, Alberta. 1981. "Cities, Capital, and Banks." In Kenneth Newton, ed. *Urban Political Economy*. New York: St. Martin's Press, pp. 200–20.

Schlozman, Kay Lehman, and John T. Tierney. 1986. *Organized Interests and American Democracy*. New York: Harper and Row.

Schmenner, Roger W. 1982. *Making Business Location Decisions*. Englewood Cliffs, NJ: Prentice Hall.

Schmitt, Eric. 1989. "Home Rule Slips in New York as Region Tackles Big Issues." *New York Times*. August 10, pp. Al, B4.

Schneider, Mark. 1985. "Suburban Fiscal Disparities and the Location Decisions of Firms." *American Journal of Political Science* 29(August, n.3):587–605.

Schultz, Stanley K. 1989. *Constructing Urban Culture: American Cities and City Planning, 1800-1920*. Philadelphia: Temple University Press.

Schumaker, Paul. 1991. *Critical Pluralism, Democratic Performance, and Community Power*. Lawrence: University Press of Kansas.

Schwartz, Nancy L. 1988. *The Blue Guitar*. Chicago: University of Chicago Press.

Sebree, Michael Monroe Kellogg. 1989. "One Century of Constitutional Home Rule." *Washington Law Review* 64(January):155–77.

Sharp, Elaine B. 1986. *Citizen Demand-Making in the Urban Context*. University: University of Alabama Press.

Shefter, Martin. 1983. "Regional Receptivity to Reform: The Legacy of the Progressive Era." *Political Science Quarterly* 98(Fall, n.3):459–83.

Smith, Robert G. 1974. *Ad Hoc Governments*. Beverly Hills, CA: Sage.

Sperow, Janice L. 1985. "Rajneeshpuram: Religion Incorporated." *Hastings Law Journal* 36:917–67.

Stark, Douglas Arthur. 1971. "Patterns of Legislator Incumbency in Independent Taxing Non-School Special Districts of California." Unpublished Ph.D. dissertation. University of Southern California.

Stein, Robert M. 1990. *Urban Alternatives: Public and Private Markets in the Provision of Local Services*. Pittsburgh: University of Pittsburgh Press.

Stetzer, Donald Foster. 1975. *Special Districts in Cook County*. Research Paper No. 169. Chicago: University of Chicago, Department of Geography.

Stone, Clarence N. 1989. *Regime Politics: Governing Atlanta, 1946–1988*. Lawrence: University Press of Kansas.

Stone, Clarence N., Robert K. Whelan, and William J. Murin. 1986. *Urban Policy and Politics in a Bureaucratic Age*, 2nd ed. Englewood Cliffs, NJ: Prentice-Hall.

Strang, David. 1985. "The Administrative Transformation of American Education: District Consolidation 1938–1980." Stanford, CA: Stanford Education Policy Institute, School of Education, Stanford University.

"Suburbs Nix Taxes." 1986. *Engineering News-Record*. December 18, p. 27.

Sumichrist, Michael, and Ronald G. Shafer. 1988. *The New Complete Book of Homebuying*. New York: Bantam.

Tableman, Betty. 1951. *Governmental Organization in Metropolitan Areas*. Ann Arbor: University of Michigan Press.

Tax Foundation, Inc. *Facts and Figures on Government Finance*, 1951, 1961, 1971, 1973, 1979, 1983. Washington, DC: The Tax Foundation.

Teaford, Jon C. 1975. *The Municipal Revolution in America: Origins of Modern Urban Government, 1650–1825*. Chicago: University of Chicago Press.

Teaford, Jon C. 1979a. *City and Suburb: The Political Fragmentation of Metropolitan America, 1850–1970*. Baltimore: Johns Hopkins University Press.

Teaford, Jon C. 1979b. "Special Legislation and the Cities, 1865–1900." *American Journal of Legal History* 23:189–212.

Teaford, Jon C. 1986. *The Twentieth-Century American City*. Baltimore: Johns Hopkins University Press.

Teaford, Jon C. 1990. *The Rough Road to Renaissance: Urban Revitalization in America, 1940–1985*. Baltimore: Johns Hopkins University Press.

Temple, David G. 1972. *Merger Politics: Local Government Consolidation in Tidewater Virginia*. Charlottesville: University Press of Virginia.

"These Businesses Tax Themselves: In the Cumberland-Galleria Area, Businesses Formed a Tax District to Cope with Rapid Growth." 1989. *Georgia Trend* 4(January, n.5, sec. 1):17.

Thompson, Dennis F. 1970. *The Democratic Citizen*. Cambridge: Cambridge University Press.

Thompson, Dennis F. 1976. *John Stuart Mill and Representative Government*. Princeton: Princeton University Press.

Tiebout, Charles M. 1956. "A Pure Theory of Local Government Expenditures." *Journal of Political Economy* 44(October):416–24.

Toll, Seymour I. 1969. *Zoned American*. New York: Grossman.

Uchitelle, Louis. 1991. "States and Cities Are Pushing Hard for Higher Taxes." *New York Times*. March 25, pp. A1, C6.

Underwood, Kathleen. 1987. *Town Building on the Colorado Frontier*. Albuquerque: University of New Mexico Press.

Urban Studies Center. 1968. "Annexation, Incorporation, and Consolidation in the Portland Metropolitan Area." Portland, OR: Urban Studies Center, Portland State College.

U.S. Bureau of Old-Age and Survivors Insurance. *County Business Patterns*, 1951, 1959. Washington, DC: U.S. Government Printing Office.

U.S. Department of Commerce. *Census of Governments*, 1952, 1957, 1962, 1967, 1972, 1977, 1982, 1987. Washington, DC: U.S. Government Printing Office.

U.S. Department of Commerce. *1970 Census of Population: Characteristics of the Population*, v.1. Washington, DC: Government Printing Office

U.S. Department of Commerce. *County and City Data Book*, 1949, 1956, 1962, 1972, 1983. Washington, DC: U.S. Government Printing Office.

U.S. Department of Commerce. *County Business Patterns*, 1970, 1981. Washington, DC: U.S. Government Printing Office.

U.S. Department of Commerce. 1987. *Government Organization Data Tape*. Washington, DC: U.S. Government Printing Office.

Verba, Sidney, and Norman H. Nie. 1972. *Participation in America*. New York: Harper and Row.

Vidich, Arthur, and Joseph Bensman. 1958. *Small Town Politics in Mass Society*. Princeton: Princeton University Press.

Walsh, Annmarie Hauck. 1978. *The Public's Business: ThePolitics and Practices of Government Corporations*. Cambridge: MIT Press.

Walzer, Norman, and David L. Chicoine. 1981. *Financing State and Local Governments in the 1980s*. Cambridge: Oelgeschlager, Gunn & Hain.

Warner, Samuel Bass. 1978. *Streetcar Suburbs*, 2nd ed. Cambridge: Harvard University Press.

Warner, Samuel Bass. 1987. *The Private City: Philadelphia in Three Periods of Its Growth*, 2nd ed. Philadelphia: University of Pennsylvania Press.

Waste, Robert J. 1983. "The Early Years in the Life Cycle of City Councils." *Urban Studies* 20:73–81.

Waste, Robert J. 1989. *The Ecology of City Policymaking*. New York: Oxford University Press.

Webb, Sidney, and Beatrice Webb. 1963. *The Development of English Local Government, 1689–1835*. London: Oxford University Press.

Weber, Adna Ferrin. 1899. *The Growth of Cities in the Nineteenth Century: A Study in Statistics*. New York: Macmillan.

Weiher, Gregory. 1989. "Public Policy and Patterns of Residential Segregation." *Western Political Quarterly* 42(December):651–77.

Weinstein, Bernard L., Harold T. Gross, and John Rees. 1985. *Regional Growth and Decline in the United States*. New York: Praeger.

Weiss, Marc A. 1987. *The Rise of the Community Builders*. New York: Columbia University Press.

Welch, Susan, and Timothy Bledsoe. 1988. *Urban Reform and Its Consequences*. Chicago: University of Chicago Press.

Westerstahl, Jorgen. 1974. "Decision-Making Systems in Thirty-Six Swedish Communes." In Terry Nichols Clark, ed. *Comparative Community Politics*. New York: Wiley, pp. 141–62.

"Westlands Water District Is a Global Laboratory." *PR Newswire*. June 28, 1989. Dateline: Fresno, CA.

Williams, Joan C. 1985. "The Invention of the Municipal Corporation: A Case Study in Legal Change." *The American University Law Review* 34:369–438.

Williams, Joan C. 1986. "The Constitutional Vulnerability of American Local Government: The Politics of City Status in American Law." *Wisconsin Law Review* 83–153.

Wilson, James Q. 1962. *The Amateur Democrat*. Chicago: University of Chicago Press.

Wilson, William Julius. 1980. *The Declining Significance of Race*, 2nd ed. Chicago: University of Chicago Press.

Wirt, Frederick M. 1970. *Politics of Southern Equality: Law and Social Change in a Mississippi County*. Chicago: Aldine.

Wood, Robert C. 1959a. "A Division of Powers in Metropolitan Areas." In Arthur Maass, ed. *Area and Power*. Glencoe, IL: Free Press.

Wood, Robert C. 1959b. *Suburbia*. Boston: Houghton Mifflin.

Wood, Robert C. 1961. *1400 Governments*. Cambridge: Harvard University Press.

Woodruff, Clinton Rogers. 1897. "The Progress of Municipal Reform." *Municipal Affairs* 1(June):303–16.

Woodward, C. Vann. 1951. *Origins of the New South, 1877–1913*. Baton Rouge: Louisiana State University Press.

Wrightson, Margaret. 1986. "Interlocal Cooperation and Urban Problems." *Urban Affairs Quarterly* 11:2261–75.

INDEX